ELIZABETH REES

CELTIC SAINTS

IN THEIR
LANDSCAPE

SUTTON PUBLISHING

First published in 2001 by
Sutton Publishing Limited · Phoenix Mill
Thrupp · Stroud · Gloucestershire · GL5 2BU

All photography by Elizabeth Rees.

Decorative motifs are taken from carved stones and artefacts in south-west Scotland
and the Isle of Man, dating from the ninth and tenth centuries.

Title-page picture: Porthgwarra Cove (see p. 169)

British Library Cataloguing in Publication Data
A catalogue record for this book is available from the British Library.

ISBN 0-7509-2686-4

Typeset in 11/15pt New Baskerville.
Typesetting and origination by
Sutton Publishing Limited.
Printed and bound in England by
J.H. Haynes & Co. Ltd, Sparkford.

CONTENTS

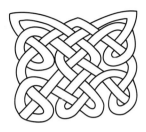

LIST OF MAPS

PREFACE

It is not easy to come close to the early British Christians, for there are few historical records from Celtic times. However, the sites where these monks and nuns lived and worked can still be visited in the more remote parts of the British Isles. Their huts, chapels and holy wells are often set in beautiful landscapes: sheltered valleys, dramatic headlands and rocky islands. Archaeology, the study of site, of place names, inscribed stones and early texts can provide us with further clues about how these men and women lived.

In this book, the reader can make an armchair tour of the sites where some fifty early British Christians worked and prayed, across Ireland, Scotland, Wales, Northumbria and Cornwall. There are several hundred more Celtic saints who do not feature in this book, and I apologise if your favourite saint is missing. This selection is biased towards those saints who chose to live in photogenic places! Most of their surviving *Lives* date from medieval times; I therefore invite the reader to view the book as 'figures in a landscape'. The figures are seen through medieval eyes, but much of the landscape remains.

I wish to thank my family for their help with the maps and proof reading, and for their facility with the computer. I am grateful to Ros Marsden for her photograph of Lindisfarne, and to the entire staff at Radstock Chemist's Shop for their patient help with developing the rest of the photographs. I have received valuable advice from Dr Jonathan Wooding of the Centre for the Study of Religion in Celtic Societies at the University of Wales, Lampeter. Thank you also to Dr Thomas O'Loughlin at Lampeter for allowing me to use his translation of St Patrick's *Confession*, published in *St Patrick, the Man and his Works* (SPCK, 1999). Any errors are my own.

My final word of thanks is to the Celtic Saints who have enticed me to meet them 'at home' in the beautiful locations where they chose to live around the shores of Britain.

Elizabeth Rees

INTRODUCTION

The ancient civilisation of the Celts flourished for over a thousand years. In the fifth century BC, Greek writers describe Celts living in the upper Danube region. It is a striking fact that when St Paul wrote to the Galatians in western Turkey, they spoke a Celtic language. This illustrates the diversity of the peoples whom the Romans encountered. The Celts conquered Rome in 386 BC and Delphi in 279 BC. They were found in Gaul and Spain, and they moved westwards from France and the Low Countries into Britain as the Germanic tribes and the Romans expanded their territories on the European mainland.

Celtic society was tribal, with elected chiefs who presided over tribal assemblies. Chiefs were also judges and commanded the army in time of war. Druids were professional teachers and priests, trained in tribal law and administration. Monks later took over much of their work. Bards were storytellers, poets and minstrels. Druids and bards appear to have become Christian priests and monks. The Celts easily absorbed Christianity: they already believed in immortality and in the sacredness of creation. It has become a cliché to say that Celtic peoples worshipped a triune god, but we still acknowledge this fact, although the Christian concept of a Trinity consisting of Father, Son and Spirit was new to these people.

Christianity entered Britain through traders and travellers, through the Roman occupation, and through Christians emigrating from Gaul. There were periodic persecutions: we hear of Alban being martyred in the third century, and of two Christian soldiers named Julius and Aaron executed at Caerleon in south-east Wales. They will be described more fully in Chapter Nine. In 313 the converted emperor Constantine gave Christians freedom to worship. A scattering of church foundations, lead cisterns for baptism and collections of Communion vessels found across Britain suggest that Christianity spread easily in later Roman times. By then there were bishops in the provincial capitals of York, London, Cirencester and Lincoln; they are recorded attending Church Councils in Gaul, Italy and Bulgaria.

In the English countryside, a number of villas became house churches, as we can tell from their wall paintings and mosaics, which depict Christian themes. When the Romans withdrew in the first decade of the fifth century, life continued in these rural communities, and a villa was sometimes the nucleus of a later village, as the word implies. Romano-British Christian families appear to have kept their faith alive. The autobiographical *Confession* of St Patrick describes a family from north or west Britain in late Roman times. Patrick tells us that his father was a deacon and that his grandfather was a priest.

In the eastern Churches of Syria, Palestine and Egypt, men and women began to move out of the cities into the desert, in order to search for God in solitude. Pilgrims from Europe returned home with stories of how they lived, and soon western men and women began to try out the monastic life for themselves. In the fourth century, Bishop Athanasius of Alexandria wrote a *Life* of the Egyptian hermit Antony. This was widely circulated, and Antony's pattern of life became a model for early monks. Athanasius relates that Antony was eighteen or twenty when his parents died. Freed from family ties, the young man then 'devoted himself to the ascetic life not far from his home, living in recollection and practising self-denial. He laboured with his own hands . . . and of what he earned, part he spent on food and part he gave to the poor.'[1]

The word 'monk' comes from the Greek term *monachos* which means 'one who is alone'. Monks lived in caves or huts, often grouped around a more experienced leader. Bishop Martin of Tours (*c.* 316–97) was the best known of the early western figures who pursued the monastic life. His friend and biographer, Sulpicius Severus, presented him as a western Antony. Martin preached widely throughout the countryside, and is likely to have provided an important model for others in the western Church. Sulpicius Severus describes how the bishop lived in a wooden cell, surrounded by about eighty disciples, who dug out caves or lived in wooden huts, and shared all they possessed.[2] The monasteries of Gaul developed a strong intellectual tradition, and from AD 400 their influence spread to Ireland and to Wales.

In Celtic kingdoms, pastoral care was tribal; parishes had not yet evolved. Many Celtic saints were high-born members of their tribe. They might be sent to a nearby monastery for a good education; later they commanded their people's respect as they spoke about their faith. Priests and bishops were married. They often lived in monasteries, alongside monks and nuns who chose to remain celibate in order to be freer to pray and preach. Monastic communities came together to share food, work and worship. Craftsmen and their families also lived around a monastic compound.

At this time, the title 'saint' simply meant someone wise and holy, or any good Christian who had died. Celtic monks and nuns, priests and bishops were often called 'saint' after their death. Many Celtic monks, particularly in Ireland, became 'pilgrims for Christ', and left home in search of a solitary place which God would show them: somewhere unknown, where they could be alone with God. Many set sail in light, hide-covered boats, drifting with the wind and currents until they reached their new location.

These men and women were not primarily missionaries, but when they settled in a new place, they had a profound impact on local people. Monks and nuns spread and flourished in the Celtic kingdoms of Ireland, Scotland and Northumbria, Wales, Cornwall and Brittany. The lives of some of the Celtic saints who lived and worked in the British Isles are examined in this book.

PART 1

IRELAND

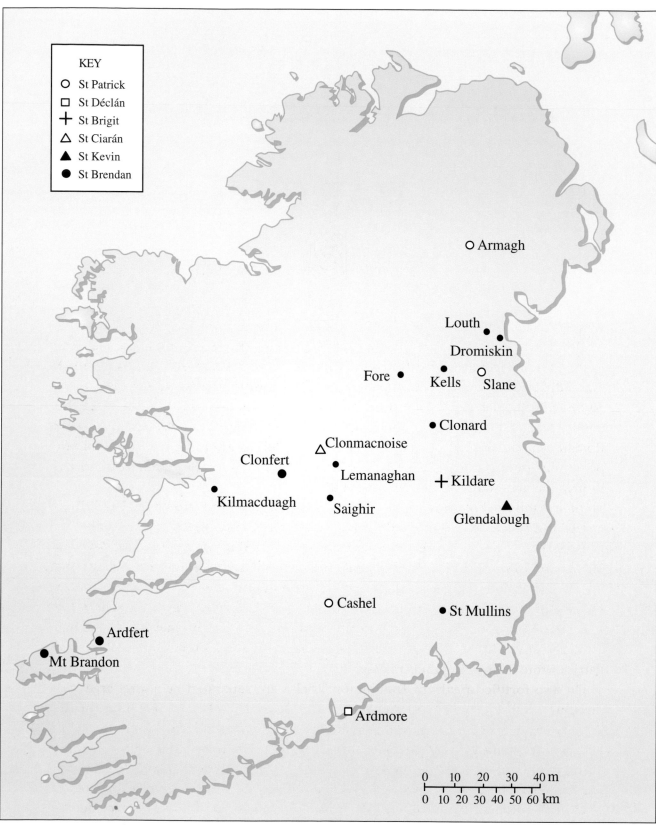

KEY

○ St Patrick
□ St Déclán
+ St Brigit
△ St Ciarán
▲ St Kevin
● St Brendan

○ Armagh

Louth
Dromiskin
Fore ● Kells ○ Slane

● Clonard

△ Clonmacnoise
Clonfert
● Lemanaghan
● + Kildare
Kilmacduagh ● Saighir ▲ Glendalough

○ Cashel ● St Mullins

● Ardfert
● Mt Brandon

□ Ardmore

0 10 20 30 40 m
0 10 20 30 40 50 60 km

Map 1: Saints of Ireland

CHAPTER ONE

PATRICK, A BRITISH MISSIONARY

Throughout Celtic times, Ireland was a centre of monastic life and learning. Christianity spread to Ireland from the Roman Empire, through families and traders from mainland Britain, Gaul and provinces further to the east. Patrick was a Briton who worked in Ireland in the fifth century. He wrote his remarkable autobiography, the *Confession*, in his old age.[1] As we have seen, he tells us that his family had taken leadership in their local church for two generations. His father was a Roman *decurion*, or civic official. Patrick does not tell us where he was born, but one possibility among others is the area of western Scotland near Dumbarton, in the Romanised area south of the Antonine Wall.

Dumbarton Rock was the capital of the British kingdom of Strathclyde. The Britons named it *Alt Clut*, or Rock of Clyde: it is a twin-peaked lava plug that towers above the Clyde estuary. The Irish referred to the stronghold as Dumbarton, meaning '*dún*, or fort, of the Britons'. Pottery and glass dating from the sixth century has been found during excavations on the Rock. According to tradition, it was the stronghold of a British chieftain named Coroticus. As an old man, Patrick wrote two letters to the soldiers of Coroticus, the second of which survives.[2] The chieftain's soldiers had raided Ireland, captured some of Patrick's converts and sold them to the Picts, and Patrick wrote demanding their release.

The two fortified peaks of Dumbarton Rock were separated by a level area with dwellings, halls, a church and a well. In 731 Bede described it as 'a town of the Britons, strongly defended to the present day'. The Vikings attacked the Rock in 870 and its inhabitants are said to have surrendered after a four-month siege. Christian Vikings buried their dead on the Rock, and there was a medieval chapel dedicated to Patrick here. The nearby town of Old Kilpatrick may even have been his birthplace. There was a Roman garrison here, above the River Clyde, on a site now occupied by the bus station. Downhill from the Roman fort, the modern church may stand on the site of a Celtic one.

In his *Confession*, Patrick tells us that when he was sixteen he was captured by Irish raiders and taken to Ireland as a slave. He writes: 'When I had arrived in Ireland and

1. Dumbarton Rock, in the Clyde estuary.

was looking after flocks the whole time, I prayed frequently each day. And more and more, the love of God and the fear of him grew in me, and my faith was increased and my spirit enlivened. So much so that I prayed up to a hundred times in the day and almost as often at night. I even remained in the wood and on the mountain to pray. And – come hail, rain or snow – I was up before dawn to pray . . . I now understand this, that the Spirit was fervent in me.'[3]

This is the most powerful and moving account we possess of the call of an early British Christian to a monastic way of life. It led Patrick to choose exile as a pilgrim for Christ. After six years he escaped or was freed, and returned home to Britain. He trained as a priest, perhaps in Gaul. Patrick felt drawn to return to Ireland as a missionary, and eventually did so. On his arrival in Ireland, he suffered hardships and was criticised and ridiculed, but he persevered, and baptised many people.[4]

Patrick's autobiography contains few names of locations, so we do not know where he worked. He tells us that he was a bishop, and he appears to have been based in the north-east, where he may have founded a settlement at Armagh. The later monks of Armagh claimed him as the founder of their cathedral, and recorded stories about Patrick which may be based on fact or may simply be ecclesiastical propaganda to promote their patron saint. Patrick's seventh-century biographer, Muirchú, describes a dramatic confrontation between the saint and the High King who lived at Tara, 25 miles north-west of Dublin. He relates how Easter that year fell on the same day as the great Celtic fire festival, when every fire had to be extinguished, until a new one was lit on Tara at dawn. Patrick gathered his followers on the nearby hill of Slane, 12 miles further north, to celebrate the resurrection of Christ by lighting the Easter fire. The furious king came to Tara and encountered Patrick, who then emerged victorious from a contest of magic with the king's bards.

Muirchú linked Patrick with Tara at a time when the Church of Armagh was forging an alliance with the rising dynasty of the Uí Néill, who used the ancient capital of Tara as a symbol of their authority. Muirchú wished to place the conversion of Ireland within a theological context: as the Israelites were delivered from their slavery to the Egyptians in a single night, and as Jesus freed the waiting dead through his resurrection on Easter night, so his servant Patrick delivered Ireland from paganism through celebrating the Easter Vigil and lighting the paschal fire. Muirchú explains that the Irish had already been prepared for this. Their wise men or magi (he uses the gospel word to describe them) had consulted their books and already knew that a powerful new teaching would come to supersede them.[5]

While there is no conclusive evidence that Patrick ever visited Slane, an early Celtic monastery associated with Bishop Erc was established on the hilltop. A saying attributed to Patrick runs:

> Bishop Erc,
> Whatever he judged was rightly judged.
> Whosoever gives a just judgement
> Shall receive the blessing of Bishop Erc.

The monastery had a round tower, which no longer survives. The Irish annals state that in 950 it was set on fire by 'foreigners from Dublin': these were Vikings. Bishop Erc's bell and staff were burnt, along with many people who had taken refuge in the tower, including the reader of the monastery. The present ruined church dates from the sixteenth century.

In his *Confession*, Patrick tells us that he travelled to the far ends of the known world in order to bring Christianity to an alien people: 'I have gone where no one else had ever gone to baptise people, ordain clergy or complete people (in their faith) . . . so that even after my death I may leave something of value to the many thousands, my brothers and sisters, sons and daughters I have baptised in the Lord.'[6] Patrick also trained priests to care for these new Christians: 'Through me . . . everywhere clerics were ordained (to serve) this people who have but recently come to belief.'[7] Patrick describes how 'the Irish leaders' sons and daughters are seen to become monks and virgins of Christ. . . . This, of course, is not to the liking of their fathers, and they have to suffer persecution and false accusation from their parents.'[8]

2. Slane: ancient gravestones outside the church.

Patrick felt called to establish Christian communities and to train others to lead them: 'It is truly our task to cast our nets and catch a great multitude and crowd for God; and (to ensure) that there are clergy everywhere to baptise and preach to a people who are in want and in need.'[9] Patrick appears to have worked in central and northern Ireland, while other early bishops were preaching in the south. In each area, it is likely that Patrick would have sought permission from the local chieftain before ministering to his people. A story relates how Patrick came to Cashel to visit the King of Munster, who agreed to be baptised. During the ceremony, Patrick accidentally pierced the king's foot with his staff. The king made no complaint, thinking that this was part of the ritual.

Cashel in County Tipperary was the chief stronghold of the kings of Munster for 900 years. Its name comes from *caisel*, an Irish word derived from the Latin *castellum*, meaning a circular stone fort. It is built on a rocky outcrop that dominates the surrounding land. Its first king was said to be Conall Corc, the son of a British mother who had returned from long exile in the land of the Picts. This may imply that Conall came from a group of Irish who had colonised parts of south Wales in *c.* 400 and who were subsequently expelled. Conall or his brother and predecessor was the king whom Patrick is said to have baptised.

It is not known how soon there was an ecclesiastical presence at Cashel, but a large church bell survives, dating from the ninth century. It is 30 centimetres high and 20 centimetres across, and is preserved in Limerick University. Seen in the photograph is a reconstruction of the bell, in the museum at Cashel. In 1101 the ruler of the fortress handed over the Rock to the Church, as the seat of the new diocese of Cashel. New buildings were constructed, including a round tower, a cathedral and a magnificent chapel built by Cormac, King of Cork and Bishop of Cashel. Cormac's chapel was consecrated in 1134.

We do not know where or how Patrick died. Our only clues are found in his *Confession*. Patrick writes: 'I was all set to go (to Britain), and wanted to go, for it is my homeland and where my family is – and (to) Gaul to visit the brethren and to see the face of my Lord's saints – God knows how much I wanted to do this.'[10] It appears that Patrick had hoped to visit his friends, perhaps the monks of Tours or Lérins, but instead he remained at his difficult task in

3. Cashel: the monastery bell.

Ireland: 'Not a day passes but I expect to be killed or waylaid or taken into slavery or assaulted in some other way. But for the sake of the promise of heaven I fear none of these things.'[11] Patrick kept faithful to the initial call that he had received as a teenager: 'The one and only purpose I had in going back to that people from whom I had earlier escaped was the gospel and the promises of God. . . . And this is my declaration before I die.'[12]

Many churches claim to have been founded by Patrick and his followers. Early sites are likely to include those whose names incorporate the Celtic word *domnach*, which was a pre-monastic word for a church. It comes from the Latin root that gives us *Dominica* ('the day of the Lord'), or Sunday. There are about thirty churches named *Domnach Patraic* scattered across northern Ireland. Others, such as Donaghmore outside Navan, honour followers of Patrick. Donaghmore (*Domnach Mór*) means 'great church', and the relics of Cassán, a follower of Patrick, were venerated there.

The monastery at Dromiskin, 5 miles south of Dundalk, is said to have been founded by a follower of Patrick named Lughaidh. Its remains include an early round tower dating from the ninth century. It has an unusually squat shape: it is only 17 metres high.

4. Round tower at Dromiskin near Dundalk.

The second abbot, Ronan, died when plague swept through Ireland in 664. There are remains of a large high cross constructed between 844 and 924, in the time of High King Finneath. The monastery was plundered by the Irish in 908, by the Danes in 978 and again by the Irish in 1043. Among Celtic peoples, tribal ties were strong, and even monks were involved in family rivalries, fighting men of other communities. However, since Dromiskin is near the coast, it was also an inviting target for Viking marauders.

Another follower of Patrick was Mochta, who died in about 534. He is mentioned by Adomnán, Abbot of Iona, who, writing in about 690, described Mochta as 'a Briton and a holy man, disciple of the holy bishop Patrick'. He was said to have first settled in County Meath and, because of local oppostion, moved northwards and established a large monastery in a settlement which was called Louth, in honour of the Celtic sun god, Lugh. A small twelfth-century church survives in Louth, known as *Teach Naomh Mochta*, or Mochta's House. It is a two-storeyed chapel with a tall roof, of a type unique to Ireland. It has a croft or attic set above an arched barrel vault, like Columba's House in Kells (see Chapter Seventeen). This design prevented the roof from collapsing inwards. A stairway leads to the upper floor beneath the roof.

5. Sunday Mass at Kilmahew, near Cardross.

Louth became a bishopric, and gave its name to County Louth. There are the remains of two medieval abbeys alongside Mochta's church: St Mary's abbey, thought to date from 1148, and that of Saints Peter and Paul founded a couple of years earlier; only a section of its wall survives. Nowadays, Louth is only a village, 4 miles north of Ardee.

In Scotland, Mochta is known as Mahew, and his church of Kilmahew is near Dumbarton at Cardross, close to the River Clyde. The church is built on a raised, oval Celtic site, and in the porch is the top of a pre-Christian standing stone. A simple cross was carved on it in the sixth century, perhaps by the Christian missionary who founded the church.[13] The long, low, whitewashed building dates from the fifteenth century; it contains its original 'sacrament house', a wooden cupboard set into the inner wall of the sanctuary. It is visible in the photograph on the previous page to the left of the priest, behind the altar.

There is a tradition that when Patrick escaped from Ireland he landed on the Lancashire coast at Heysham, which overlooks Morecambe Bay, before travelling north to rejoin his family, and in the eighth century, a tiny chapel dedicated to Patrick was built on the headland. It is more likely, however, that missionaries came here after

6. Cliff-top shrine at Heysham.

Patrick's death. No evidence of a monastery has been found on the headland, but carved into the rock at each end of the oratory are sixth-century repositories for bones, six in a row on one side, with others lower down the slope. The cavities are too small for graves. Each has a rim to take a lid, and a socket at its head, into which a cross was inserted. Others brought their dead for burial in this holy place. The bodies of ninety Vikings and later Christians have been found in and around the chapel, near the shrines of the monks.

The chapel on the headland was decorated with yellow, red, white and green-brown wall plaster. Traces of both paintings and lettering were found. In the chapel was a ceremonial stone chair or throne. One of its arms was discovered, shaped like a bird's head, with prominent eyes and a hooked beak; this can be seen in the museum at Lancaster. The stone blocks which form the chapel walls are held together by mortar made with burnt sea shells for lime, poured between the stones while it was still hot. This was a style used by the Romans. The tall, narrow building was extended by the Saxons in the tenth century. Its new doorway was decorated with a ribbed arch.

An ancient stone passage leads downhill from St Patrick's chapel and its graveyard to a flat, sheltered spot where the parish church of St Peter stands. If there was a monastery, it may have been here. The base of an elaborate Anglian cross stands in the churchyard; carved on its north face is a roofed structure with windows framing the heads of Saints. Anglians settled in this area of Britain in the sixth and seventh centuries. The church was rebuilt in the mid-tenth century as a barn-like building with small stone doorways, two of which survive. A fine Viking hogback tombstone also dates from this time. It is shaped like a feasting hall, with an animal's head at each end of its gabled roof. Along each side is a procession of creatures and people. Further north, visible from the M6, the church of Preston Patrick is also said to mark Patrick's journey northwards, but this is likely to be a medieval legend.

CHAPTER TWO

DÉCLÁN, PRINCE OF ARDMORE

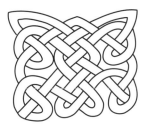

There were a number of missionaries preaching in south-east Ireland in the early fifth century, before Patrick began working in the north. One of these was Déclán of Ardmore. We know a little about him because a twelfth-century *Life of Déclán* survives.[1] This relates that he was a prince of the Déisi, a tribe which had been expelled from Tara. The story of their wanderings was told by the Irish bards. Some of the clan returned to Tara, some migrated to Wales, and others found a home in south-east Ireland, after an intertribal marriage. Here, Déclán was born at Lismore. According to his *Life*, there were already Christians in the area, and a priest named Colmán came to his parents' home and baptised their son. Following Celtic custom, Déclán was fostered by his uncle. At the age of seven he was sent to a holy man, and learnt to read, write and pray. Déclán also went abroad to study, perhaps to Wales or Gaul, and returned with his monk's bell and staff.

In about 416, Déclán established a community at Ardmore on the south coast, halfway between Cork and Waterford. *Ard mór* means 'great height', and Déclán chose a site on fertile high ground overlooking a sandy bay. The headland may then have been an island in the mouth of the River Blackwater, before it burst its banks in 803 and made a new channel to the sea through Youghal Bay. A cluster of Roman and early Christian remains has been found in the Blackwater valley, including a number of ogham-inscribed stones. These remains provide a context for Déclán's life and work. From his monastery at Ardmore, Déclán travelled among the Déisi, preaching, baptising and building churches. He journeyed further north and preached to King Aongus at Cashel. The king refused baptism because his clan were not on good terms with the Déisi, but he allowed Déclán to work among his people.

The ruined cathedral at Ardmore dates from the ninth century. Inside its chancel, two ogham-inscribed grave markers date from near to Déclán's lifetime. The ogham stroke alphabet was devised by Irish Latin-speaking intellectuals, perhaps as early as AD 300.[2] It uses the sound-values of spoken Latin and consists of incised lines grouped along two adjacent sides of a stone slab. Strokes were easier to carve than the rounded letters of the Latin alphabet. Most of these early memorial stones are found in south-east Ireland, in Munster and Leinster; some are inscribed both in ogham and Latin. Christians travelling to Wales and Cornwall brought with them the custom of erecting ogham-inscribed stones. A bilingual ogham and Latin grave marker is reproduced in Chapter Nineteen.

7. Ogham-inscribed gravestone, Ardmore.

By the twelfth century when Déclán's *Life* came to be written, little was known about his work, and the adventures recounted in his biography may have little basis in fact. However, there were traditions about Déclán's love of solitude, and his choice of a 'desert' or place of retreat on the headland 800 metres beyond the monastery. Here was his hermitage, in a sheltered spot beside a spring. In old age, he was said to have moved out of the monastic 'city' in order to come and live here. Déclán's *Life* relates: 'He lived at that time in a narrow place close to the sea, where a shining stream flows down from the hills above. It is surrounded by trees and bushes, and is called *Déclán's Desert*. From there, the (monastic) city is about a mile distant, and Déclán went there to avoid noise, so that he could pray and fast there.'[3]

Déclán's Desert is still a peaceful place surrounded by bushes and trees. In the early morning one can look out across the sparkling sea and watch fishermen in the bay, far below. There are remains of a large ruined church: its east end is from the fourteenth century but its west end, seen in the photograph, is earlier. Beyond the ruined church is Déclán's holy well (see overleaf). Between the desert and the monastic city, on the beach, a large erratic boulder is named Déclán's Stone. It balances on two smaller rocks, and is held to cure rheumatism if one crawls beneath it. In any case, the act of doing so loosens stiff joints!

The well pool lies west of the ruined church in Déclán's Desert. Two small doorways lead down to the spring, where it is possible to bathe. The well-house is capped with two late medieval crosses, each bearing a figure of Christ. The well was restored in 1798 and again in 1951. It is visited by countless people, particularly during the week nearest to Déclán's feast day, 24 July. Up to the late 1940s, pilgrims came to spend all night in a prayer vigil at the well.

8. Déclán's Desert, Ardmore.

An account from around 1840 describes the scene on Déclán's feast day: 'The crowd then formed a long line winding up the narrow path that leads along the mountain's brow to St Déclán's chapel. . . . The scenery was beautiful as we looked over the precipitous cliffs across the bay of Ardmore. On the brink stands the remnant of a chapel, said to be the first built in Ireland. On entering the gate, on your right hand is the well St Déclán blessed. Then they knelt down and said their prayers. . . . At twenty different periods, I counted the people as they passed. They averaged fifty-five a minute, which gives a total of twelve or fifteen thousand persons.'[4] Déclán is still one of Ireland's most popular local saints, and his name is commonly given to boys.

The twelfth-century *Life of Déclán* relates that when he sensed death approaching, he returned from his hermitage to the community, to die among his brother monks. We read: 'When Déclán realised that his last days were at hand, he called for Mac Liag from the eastern Déisi, in order to receive the last sacraments from him. He foreknew the day of his death, and asked to be brought back to his own (monastic) city. . . . He was carried back to his city; Mac Liag gave him the last sacraments. He blessed all his

9. Holy well, Déclán's Desert.

people, and when he died, he was buried with honour in the tomb which he had already chosen.'[5]

The chapel of Déclán's Grave is the oldest building of the monastery, although it was restored in the eighteenth century. It is a small rectangular building on eighth-century foundations, built into the hillside on the edge of the site, where the land slopes down to the sea. Large stone blocks form the lower courses of its walls; its projecting pillars, or antae, would have supported the roof timbers. Generations of Christians have scooped out earth from Déclán's grave inside the chapel, as it is believed to protect from disease.

The round tower and the ruined west end of the cathedral at Ardmore date from the twelfth century. A number of fine but badly weathered Romanesque reliefs have been reassembled and set into the cathedral's west wall; they depict Adam and Eve, the adoration of the infant Christ by the three wise men, and other scenes.

The round tower was one of the latest to be built in Ireland. Beautifully proportioned, it rises to a height of 29 metres. Its four tapering storeys are separated by projecting string courses, each resembling a rope. The round-arched doorway is

10. Chapel of Déclán's Grave, Ardmore.

11. Round tower and ruined cathedral, Ardmore.

4 metres above ground level. An unusual feature of the tower is that inside are projecting stones carved with grotesque heads.

Towers served as lookout posts and landmarks, guides for sailors and travellers on land. Books, chalices and shrines could be safely stored here, and monks could take refuge in the tower. This one is so strong that it withstood an attack with cannon fire when it was held by the Confederates in 1642, at a time when the native Catholic population struggled against their English Protestant overlords, and Oliver Cromwell ruthlessly repressed the Irish Rebellion. The elegant tower now dominates a peaceful landscape once more.

CHAPTER THREE

BRIGIT OF KILDARE

Many traditions have come down to us about the life of St Brigit, but few certain facts. She is believed to have been born some 30 miles west of Dublin, near Kildare, where she later founded a monastery. She lived a couple of generations after Patrick, and perhaps died around 525. An early Irish *Life of Brigit* describes her travelling around the countryside in a chariot. Its driver was a priest who could baptise the people to whom they preached. Kildare means 'place of the oak': Brigit established her community beside this holy tree, which survived until the tenth century. The monastery soon grew in importance, and Brigit's early *Lives* were written to enhance the monastery's fame.

In about 650, a monk named Cogitosus wrote a biography of Brigit that provides us with a valuable description of Kildare a hundred years after her death. He speaks of a double community of monks and nuns presided over by an abbess. He tells us of an elaborately decorated wooden church which contained the shrines of Brigit and Conleth, a hermit and metal worker whom Brigit invited to make church vessels for the monastery, and to be pastor of the surrounding people. The two shrines, one to the left and the other to the right of the altar were adorned with precious metals and gems. There were crowns of gold and silver hanging above them, and the church also contained images, paintings and partition walls made of boards.[1] Brigit's relics were still venerated when Kildare was raided by Danes in 836.

Little survives of the Celtic monastery at Kildare except the remains of a high cross and a round tower. Just south of the thirteenth-century cathedral, the foundations of a small rectangular building were uncovered in 1996. Now named the Fire Temple, this may have contained the convent's communal hearth. A street beside the cathedral is still called Fire Temple Lane. When Gerald of Wales visited Brigit's convent in the twelfth century, he saw a fire which the nuns carefully tended. He wrote: 'the fire is surrounded by a circular withy hedge, which men are not allowed to enter.' Brigit owes her name to Brígh, a Celtic goddess of fire and light, and inherited some of her attributes. Seen in the photograph overleaf is a carved stone slab from the monastery.

12. Carved stone, Kildare monastery.

Kildare Cathedral is set on a low ridge where six roads meet, and Brigit's monastic 'city' became a large one. In the seventh century, Cogitosus described it as 'the chief of almost all the Irish churches'. He added that the king's treasury was in Kildare, and the cathedral must have been worth plundering, for it was raided by Vikings sixteen times. Kildare seems to have been singled out for its wealth, for it was pillaged more frequently than other Irish monasteries. This suggests a steady flow of pilgrims, who donated generous gifts to Brigit's shrine. Gerald of Wales describes a fine illuminated manuscript which he called the *Book of Kildare*; it no longer survives.

One of the ancient roads leading to Kildare passes through Tully, a mile south of the city. Here is Brigit's well, and the site of the convent's water-mill. There is no stream in Kildare, and running water was necessary to turn a mill wheel, in order to grind the community's flour. The well is still a place of pilgrimage; it can be found off a signed road opposite the Irish National Stud. Brigit's well is at the far end of a small meadow; its water flows through a pool, where a stone trough and seats on either side allow pilgrims to bathe. Beside the well, a larch tree is hung with clouties, symbolic of prayers for healing.

A closer look at the cloutie tree beside Brigit's well indicates the kinds of cures for which she is invoked: bandages and handkerchiefs, socks and stockings, and children's toys form silent prayers for healing broken limbs, crippled feet and sick children. Close to the trunk is a wooden rosary: its beads are used in a repeated prayer to Our Lady. Brigit became a patroness of healers, midwives and newborn babies. She was also invoked to protect cattle and to bless their milk. In medieval iconography, a cow lies at Brigit's feet.

While collecting songs in the Scottish Highlands in the nineteenth century, Alexander Carmichael recorded a large number of blessing songs invoking Brigit (who was often known as Bride) to keep herds from straying, to protect horses and sheep, to preserve the peat fire, to mend broken bones and to bring peaceful sleep.[2] In a culture in which childbirth could be hazardous, Brigit was often invoked to aid a healthy delivery. She took over many of these powers from Brígh, the goddess whose festival of Imbolc was celebrated on the first day of February, at the time when ewes come into milk. This later became Brigit's feast day. In an Irish custom recorded on her festival, the wooden spoon for stirring the butter churn was addressed as 'Little Bride'. It was clothed in a child's dress and decorated with a straw cross called 'Little

13. Brigit's well, Tully.

14. Cloutie tree, Brigit's well.

Bride's star'. Pins and needles, crystalline stones and pieces of straw were offered to Little Bride as gifts, and mothers brought her food.[3]

The custom of fashioning Brigit's cross out of rushes is widespread and ancient. A story to explain its origin relates that Brigit was called to the bedside of a dying pagan chieftain. As she sat beside him, she picked up some rushes from the floor and began to weave them into a cross. He watched her and asked what she was doing, and she told him the gospel story. Before he died, he was converted and baptised. Crosses are fashioned on St Brigit's day and put in the rafters of homes, to protect them from harm throughout the year. However, Brigit's cross is likely to pre-date Christianity, since its earlier form has three arms, not four. Brigit's cross is often hung over the byre to bless the cows, for Brigit was the patroness of cattle, as was Brígh before her. The Celts were a pastoral people, and cattle were precious possessions.

15. Brigit's cross of rushes, Tully.

The woven cross of rushes is an Irish variant of the corn dolly, a shrine in which the corn spirit was seen to reside as a life-giving presence in the home. The word 'dolly' (or 'little idol') is an ancient name for an image or representation. Throughout Europe and the Near East, corn dollies of various designs have been hung in homes, barns and churches, as a symbol of blessing and a prayer that crops will flourish.[4] Brigit's connection with the fertility of crops, cattle and children is another indication of the fusion of her cult with that of a pre-Christian goddess.

In his travels through the Scottish Highlands and Islands, Carmichael noted the importance of Brigit in people's lives. In Uist, the flocks were counted and dedicated to Brigit on her feast day, which was considered to be the first day of spring. In Barra, lots were cast for the fishing banks on Brigit's day; these stretches of water were divided afresh among the fishermen each year. Carmichael records how girls in the Outer Hebrides fashioned a corn sheaf into the shape of a woman on the eve of Brigit's feast. They decorated the figure with shells, bright pebbles, snowdrops and primroses which flower in the mild Hebridean winters. The girls dressed in white and visited each house for people to give them bannocks, cheese and butter. The young men and women feasted, sang and danced through the night. At dawn they formed a circle and sang a hymn to Brigit, and then distributed the food which they had collected to poor women in the neighbourhood.[5]

In Carmichael's *Carmina Gadelica* (or 'Gaelic Songs'), he recorded chants sung at Brigit's festival to invoke her power. Their names illustrate their protective function: 'Bride's Breastplate', 'Bride's Mantle', 'Bride's Shield' and 'Bride's Staff'. Because she was invoked in childbirth, a story arose that she was Mary's midwife at the birth of Jesus. Brigit was invoked as 'aid-woman of Mary' and 'foster mother of Christ'. In ancient cultures, midwives were highly honoured, and fostership was considered a close and tender tie. A Highland proverb runs: 'Blood to the twentieth, fostership to the hundredth degree.' In a baptism rite from the Highlands, the midwife dedicated the newborn child to the Trinity by letting three drops of clear cold water fall on its forehead, as she recalled Brigit's delivery of the child Jesus.

On the eve of Brigit's feast (which was 13 February according to the old calendar), Carmichael watched older women construct a basket or cradle which they called 'Bride's bed'. After decorating it, they took a sheaf of oats and fashioned a corn dolly in the shape of a woman, which they called 'Brigit's icon' (or *dealbh Bride* in Gaelic). They decorated it with flowers, strips of cloth, white shells and pebbles. In a simple ceremony, the corn dolly was welcomed into the home and placed in Brigit's cradle. Beside the dolly they put a small, straight white wand, with its bark peeled away. It was cut from a holy tree, such as broom, bramble or white willow. It resembled the wand or sceptre given to Irish kings at their coronation and to Lords of the Isles at their instatement. It was straight to symbolise justice, and white as an emblem of peace.[6]

Abernethy, 6 miles south-east of Perth (see map 3), is an early Christian settlement dedicated to Brigit. According to the *Pictish Chronicle*, St Bride's church at Abernethy was founded in the mid-fifth century. A note upon the chronicle relates that when King Nechtán was driven from his land by his brother Drust, he visited Brigit in Ireland and asked her to pray for him. Nechtán was restored to his kingdom, and three years later Darlugdach, Abbess of Kildare, came to Britain as an exile for Christ. After a further two years, Nechtán offered Abernethy to God and St Brigit. During the Mass of consecration, Darlugdach 'sang Alleluia over the offering'[7]. Abernethy became the principal seat of the southern Picts, with a Celtic bishop. A stone church was built by King Gartnaith in about 590. The Irish-style round tower (see overleaf) was constructed in the eleventh century, one of only two in Scotland. Abernethy remained a Celtic bishopric until about 1273, when government from Rome was introduced.

The goddess Brígh appears to have been the titular deity of the Brigantes, the largest confederacy of tribes in Britain. This was the dominant tribe in northern England before the arrival of the Romans. The Brigantes were also found in Switzerland near Lake Constance, where the town of Bregenz is named after them.[8] The Celtic word *brigā* means 'high one' or 'high place'. Living in their hill-forts, the Brigantes were successful warriors, and those whom they defeated coined the word 'brigand' to describe their unwelcome presence.

16. Round tower, Abernethy, Scotland.

There are three early church dedications to Brigit near the Somerset coast; at these sites, Brígh may formerly have been honoured. One of these is on a low hill at Chelvey, 8 miles south-west of Bristol. Another is St Bridget's church at the foot of Brean Down, 2 miles south of Weston-super-Mare. Brean is another name derived from the Celtic word *brigā*. Until medieval times, Brean Down was an island, on which people lived, farmed and worshipped for 4,000 years. In the fourth century there was a Romano-Celtic temple on the Down, with a cemetery on its lower slope. It may be that Brígh was honoured on Brean Down before Brigit was commemorated in the church below.

Five miles south-east of Brean Down, a third 'high place' named Brent Knoll rises above the marshes. Early forms of the word Brent again derive from the word *brigā*. There is a hill-fort on the summit of Brent Knoll, in which early excavations indicated a temple where Brígh may have been honoured.[9] In the settlement below, one of a line of springs was formerly known as 'Our Lady's well'; this title often refers to Brigit. Her cult is one of the clearest examples of the fusion of a Christian saint with elements of earlier religious belief.

17. Brent Knoll, Somerset.

CHAPTER FOUR

CiARÁN OF CLONMACNOISE

Ciarán of Clonmacnoise was a man of great promise who died young. Lives of the saint written centuries later describe him as the son of an Ulsterman who had settled in Connaght. Their authors record that, unlike many Irish abbots, Ciarán was not of noble birth. They indicate that he was a holy man by stating that, like Jesus, Ciarán was a carpenter's son and died at the age of thirty-three. He was said to have studied under Finnian of Clonard (see Chapter Seven), with Enda on the Aran Islands and later still with Senan on Scattery Island in the mouth of the Shannon. A story set in his student days at Clonard reflects the later importance of his own monastery: while Ciarán was reading his copy of Matthew's Gospel, a poorer student asked to borrow the book. Ciarán had studied only the first half, but lent it to him at once. Next day in class, Ciarán could answer questions only on the first half of the text, and his companions joked about 'Ciarán half-Matthew'. Abbot Finnian commented, 'Not Ciarán half-Matthew but Ciarán half-Ireland, for he will have half of Ireland and ourselves the other half'.

Ciarán founded a community on an island in Lough Ree, further north on the Shannon, before settling at Clonmacnoise, whose name means 'water meadows of the sons of Nós'. Ciarán selected a key point on the broad river, near the Athlone ford and on the sandy esker ridge that forms the great east–west road across central Ireland. Today, passing boats are a reminder that the Shannon, Ireland's longest river, was a major route north and south, so Clonmacnoise was at the main crossroads of Ireland. The water meadows flood annually and provide rich pasture that could support a large community. Annals compiled at Clonmacnoise describe its foundation by Ciarán in the 540s, on land given to him by Diarmaid Mac Cerbhaill of the royal house of Uí Néill. Diarmaid helped to build the first wooden church with his own hands, and soon afterwards became high king. Within a year, Ciarán had died of the Yellow Plague, which swept through Ireland and decimated many communities.

The photograph overleaf shows the north-west corner of the monastic compound. In the foreground is a replica of one of Ireland's finest high crosses, referred to in the annals as 'the Cross of the Scriptures'. Its shaft and head were carved from a single piece of sandstone, and an inscription round its base asks prayers for King Flann and for Abbot

18. Clonmacnoise, beside the Shannon.

Colmán who made it. Colmán was abbot from about 904 to 926, and erected the largest of the churches on the site. Behind the cross stands a ruined round tower. Annalists recorded its completion in 1124. However, storms caused damage in the following decades: in 1135 the top of the tower was struck off by lightning. In 1149 St Ciarán's yew tree was also felled by lightning, and 113 sheep sheltering beneath it were killed.

Little survives from Ciarán's monastery. Pieces of sixth-century pottery have been found, and in 1990 an ogham-inscribed gravestone was discovered, perhaps dating from the fifth or sixth century. It is the first to have been found in this region of Ireland; later it was used for sharpening iron tools. It lay beneath the new graveyard, at the eastern end of the monastic site. Further excavation uncovered a roadway, traces of houses, corn-drying kilns and a boat slip. At the opposite end of the site, beyond the round tower, underwater excavation carried out in 1994–8 uncovered the remains of a wooden bridge across the Shannon. Tree-ring dating of its oak timbers suggests that it was built in about 804.[1]

Near the centre of the compound is the smallest of the churches, Temple Ciarán. According to tradition, Ciarán was buried here, and pilgrims used to take home soil from the grave to heal their sick. A relic known as St Ciarán's Hand was kept here until 1684, when the chapel was still roofed. The early tenth-century building has putlog holes in its walls: these held timbers to which scaffolding was tied during the chapel's construction. Its walls are no longer vertical, since so many burials around the founder's tomb have caused the earth to shift.

The photograph is of the South Cross, carved in the ninth century. A damaged inscription on its base suggests that it was commissioned by the father of King Flann, who is mentioned on the Cross of the Scriptures. Both these sandstone crosses were probably quarried in County Clare, transported up the Shannon, and carved here in the monastic workshops. Much of the South Cross is covered with abstract ornament, in the form of interlacing and fretwork, spirals and bosses. This style of decoration appears to derive from earlier metal-encased wooden crosses. The elaborate bosses echo the shapes and patterns found on metalwork and jewellery of the period.[2]

Despite Ciarán's early death, Clonmacnoise grew rapidly in importance. Adomnán wrote in his *Life of Columba* (*c.* 690) that when Alither was abbot of Clonmacnoise, Columba paid him a visit. He relates: 'When they heard of his approach, everyone in the fields near the monastery came from all directions. Together with those inside the monastery, they most eagerly accompanied their abbot, Alither. They passed beyond the enclosure wall of the property and with one accord they went to meet St Columba, as if he were an angel of the Lord.'[3] Adomnán hints here that Iona was rather more important than Clonmacnoise!

By the seventh century, Clonmacnoise had a large non-monastic population, and had acquired many dependent

19. The South Cross, Clonmacnoise.

churches. This led to disputes over property. In about 700, Tírechán, the biographer of Patrick, complained that the community of Clonmacnoise forcibly held many churches that had been founded by Patrick. In spite of their rapturous welcome of Columba, a further dispute arose between the monks of Clonmacnoise and those of Columba's foundation at Durrow, 35 miles south-east. Monks from the two communities fought each other in 764, and two hundred men from Durrow were killed.[4]

There was intensive settlement around the monastery, with circular houses where artisans lived with their families: metalworkers in iron and bronze, gold and silver, and craftsmen skilled in antler working or comb-making. There were also stone masons who, besides carving crosses, produced some seven hundred grave markers over a period of four hundred years. A piece of scratched bone that was used by an apprentice to practise plaitwork patterns still survives. His attempts were rather unskilled! The photograph is of a reconstruction of a monastic altar. Beneath a woven hanging, two chalices can be seen, with a wine strainer, and a patten, or dish for the bread. Behind an illuminated missal is a small house-shaped reliquary; to the left is a bronze bell.

Since Ciarán was not of noble birth and his family were not native to the area, he left no dynasty from which abbots might be chosen. His family was not represented among later abbots, and the monastery remained independent of other clans. Chroniclers in

20. Reconstruction of a monastic altar, Clonmacnoise.

21. Temple Finghin, Clonmacnoise.

the community kept records of significant events from at least the eighth century, and it is possible to compile an almost complete list of abbots from Ciarán's time until the twelfth century. The settlement's churches were burnt down more than thirty times during this period by accident, by Irish kings and by Viking raiders.

Monks in the scriptorium must have illuminated fine gospel books, but none have survived. However, the ornate metalwork shrine of the *Stowe Missal* (*c.* 1030) bears an inscription stating that it was crafted by a monk of Clonmacnoise. Some secular texts written by the monks have been preserved, including the *Book of the Dun Cow*, which contains the earliest known version of the *Cattle Raid of Cooley* (or *Táin Bó Cuailnge*), a popular Irish saga.

The annals record that in 1013, the great oak of Finghin's churchyard was blown down in a storm. Temple Finghin is on the northern boundary of the enclosure, exposed to winds whipping across the meadowland from the Shannon below. The ruined stone church on the site has a unique belfry which also served as a round tower. With such frequent raids, the monks may have felt the need for this second tower into which they could hurry for protection. The belfry is set at the junction of

22. The Nuns' Church, Clonmacnoise.

the chancel and the nave; its conical cap is well preserved.

One of the main approach roads to the monastery from the east leads past the Nuns' Church. It continues through the graveyard, where its large stone slabs have been named the Pilgrims' Way. On a gravel ridge to the right of the road, halfway to the Nuns' Church, a small platform of stones appears to be the Cairn of the Three Crosses which monks mention in the annals. In summer the grass here is bright with purple orchids and other flowers. In 1026 a chronicler describes the construction of a causeway from the piglets' yard to the Cross of Congal. We learn other details: in 1104, the cathedral roof was covered with wooden slates. A collection of treasures was stolen from the high altar in 1129 by a Scandinavian plunderer. He was tracked down in Limerick the following year and hanged by the king of Munster, and the monks recovered their treasures.

The Nuns' Church and its cemetery is half a kilometre east of the main site, within its own enclosure. According to the chronicles, in the cemetery was a stone church which was burnt down in 1082. Its remains are incorporated into an adjoining field wall. The annals relate that the present church was completed in 1167 by Dearbhforgaill, wife of the king of Breifne. The overking of Leinster abducted her during a raid, and apparently she was not unwilling to be captured.

The monastic chronicler records with disapproval how the king of Leinster 'kept her for a long time to satisfy his insatiable, carnal and adulterous lust', before returning her the following year. Her husband later drove the king of Leinster into exile, but the overking sought help from Henry II of England, and thus the Anglo-Norman invasion began. In 1186, at the mature age of seventy-eight, Queen Dearbhforgaill retired to the Cistercian abbey of Mellifont, where she died seven years later.[5]

CHAPTER FIVE

KEVIN OF GLENDALOUGH

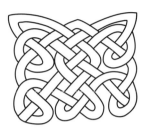

Kevin was a contemporary of Ciarán of Clonmacnoise. Each founded a settlement beside an important routeway, and both monasteries later grew in size and importance. But while Clonmacnoise overlooks flat meadows and the broad, winding Shannon, Glendalough is in very different terrain, beside a pass through the Wicklow Mountains. Its name, *Gleann-dá-loch*, means 'Glen of the two lakes', and it is set in an outstandingly beautiful location, 25 miles south of Dublin and 12 miles inland. The surviving *Lives* of Kevin are unreliable and late, so we know little about him, but unlike Ciarán, he appears to have lived well into old age. His Latin *Life* describes Kevin travelling west across Ireland to visit Ciarán at Clonmacnoise as the young man lay stricken with the plague, but Ciarán died before the older monk's arrival. There are remains of a church dedicated to Ciarán at Glendalough; the two communities developed links in the tenth century.

Kevin (d. *c.* 618) was born in the early sixth century, of a noble Leinster family ousted from kingship. His name Cóemhghein means 'fairborn'. There are six surviving *Lives* of Kevin, three in Latin and three in Irish. The earliest appears to have been written by a monk at Glendalough in the tenth or eleventh century, since he refers to Dublin as a powerful and warlike city of men who were hardy fighters and most skilful with ships; this describes a city under Viking control. We do not know where Kevin was educated; he was said to have been trained by three wise old monks. The *Life* describes Kevin searching for a deserted place to live and pray. He came to Glendalough and lived beside the Upper Lake in the hollow of a tree. Later he was ordained a priest by a bishop named Lugidus, who sent him out with some monks to found a new church in an unidentified place. Here he spent some time 'gathering servants for Christ' before moving with them to Glendalough.

According to his Latin *Life*, Kevin founded a great monastery in the lower part of the valley where two clear rivers flow together. Once the community was established, he entrusted it to the care of responsible monks and retired to the upper valley, a mile to the west, to live once more as a hermit. Here he built a small dwelling in a narrow place between the mountain and the lake, where there were dense woods

Left: 23. Dawn on the Upper Lake, Glendalough.

Opposite: 24. Early graves, Reefert churchyard, Glendalough.

and clear streams. This area is known as *Díseart Kevin* (Kevin's Desert). In the photograph above, the early morning sun begins to warm the south-eastern corner of the Upper Lake, where Kevin built his 'desert' or hermitage. He was said to have fed on sorrel and nettles. Beside the shore, sorrel of unusually fine quality still grows; nettle broth was considered a valuable food at this time, and sorrel soup is still much prized.

On a promontory overlooking the Upper Lake, the remains of a circular hut known as Kevin's Cell have been excavated, and there are possible sites of other huts further up the hillside. There is an early church, *Temple na Skellig*, on a shelf above the Upper Lake, close to 'St Kevin's Bed', a cave in the rock face which may have been a Bronze Age mine-shaft.[1] According to tradition, Kevin used this as a shelter. The Poulanass river cascades down the hillside into the Upper Lake on its southern shore, and not far from the river is the Reefert church, in a grove of hazel trees. This appears to have been a church used by the solitary monks who chose to live in Kevin's Desert. When a number of monks withdrew to a 'desert' away from the main monastic site, a superior might be appointed to take charge of their settlement.

The Reefert church is a fine eleventh-century building with an early example of a chancel arch. A large stone with four interlinked crosses may have been an altar front; it is now in St Kevin's church in the monastic city. The graveyard is one of the few in which Celtic grave markers are still in their original position, lying flat on the graves, with other slabs and small crosses serving as upright headstones.[2] An inscription on one tombstone reads: 'A prayer for Caibre, son of Cathail.' According to the annals, Caibre was a hermit of Glendalough who died in 1013. The name Reefert appears to derive from '*Righ Fearta*', or 'burial place of kings'. The title may date from the late twelfth century when the royal family of the O'Tooles were driven from Kildare into the Wicklow Mountains by the Normans. Reefert was known as the Princes' Church in the eighteenth century.

After some years as a hermit beside the Upper Lake, Kevin apparently returned to the monastic city to die. His *Life* relates that he sent a party of monks to the hermitage to pray for him. It describes his burial place, 'to the east of the Lower Lake'. This appears to indicate St Mary's church, at the western end of the monastic city. This is one of the earliest churches on the site; in the eighteenth century it was still venerated as the place of Kevin's burial. Its chancel was probably built in the tenth century, but its nave is considerably earlier. After his death, Kevin was succeeded as abbot by his nephew Molibba, who appears to have been the first bishop of Glendalough.

In the foreground of the photograph is the River Glendasan, near its confluence with the River Glenealo. The monastery is set on higher ground, above the two streams. It is a common opinion that the monks moved to this location only after Kevin's death, but it is equally possible that Kevin chose this site. As we have seen, Kevin's *Life* describes the original foundation 'where two clear rivers flow together', at a distance from Kevin's Desert.[3] The earlier monk Déclán retired to a desert a mile away from the community at Ardmore, returning to his brother monks in order to die among them (see Chapter Two).

The lower site at Glendalough is extensive, with remains of five churches and a round tower. Another two churches were later built further down the valley. The main entrance to the monastery is close to the road where it crosses the Glendasan River. The present bridge may stand on the site of an earlier one which the annals describe as being swept away in the great flood of 1177. The enclosure is approached by a gateway, the only surviving monastic entrance in Ireland. The impressive building dates from some time after 900. Two fine granite arches survive; its antae, or projecting walls at each end, suggest that there was a timber roof. The outline of a large, simple cross is carved on a giant slab beyond the inner arch. This marked out the monastery as a place of sanctuary, where criminals could take refuge from the law. Beneath the arches are preserved the large paving slabs of the original causeway into the monastic city.

Opposite. 25. Glendalough: the monastery seen from the river.

In time the monastery would have contained workshops, scriptoria for manuscript writing and copying, guest-houses and an infirmary, farm buildings and dwellings both for monks and for craftsmen and labourers, together with their families. The site was above flood level and on fertile soil, with woodland bordering the Glenealo river to the south. The hillside is named Derrybawn, from the Gaelic for 'white oak wood'. The white-leaved oak was particularly revered. It also provided valuable fuel, and oak was durable timber for building. The oak galls may have been used to make black ink, and herds of pigs from the monastery would have foraged for acorns. Wild garlic growing on the grassy woodland banks was used in cooking.

26. St Kevin's church, Glendalough.

St Kevin's church is the best preserved building within the enclosure. Its steeply pitched stone roof is built on the corbel principle, like the beehive huts of Kerry; each stone slopes slightly outwards to throw off the rain. It is similar in construction to Columba's house in Kells (see Chapter Seventeen). In each, there is a first floor with a small croft above, in which monks may have slept. In St Kevin's church there are holes for beams which supported the first floor, 3.8 metres above ground level. A small round tower is built into the west gable; a similar belfry was constructed at Trinity church, further down the valley, but it collapsed during a storm in 1818.

The small sacristy adjoining St Kevin's church was perhaps built in the twelfth century, when a chancel was also added. In 1779 when the antiquarian Gabriel Béranger visited the site, there was a small altar of stones and sods in the chancel. Eucharist was celebrated here during the 'Pattern' or patronal feast of Kevin on 3 June. From about 1810, Sunday Mass was held here. The chancel was later destroyed; its foundations are visible beside the sacristy.[4]

North of St Kevin's church is a small building known as the Priests' House, since priests were buried here in the eighteenth and nineteenth centuries. Set over its doorway is an early carved stone depicting a robed, seated abbot. To his left an attendant holds a crozier; to his right, a stooping monk rings a hand-bell. At the centre of the monastic city is the cathedral, a large building constructed over several hundred years from the ninth century onwards. It is referred to in the annals as 'the

27. Round tower at dawn, Glendalough.

abbey', and was an imposing building: its nave is wider than that of any other early Irish church. Outside it stands a tall ringed cross of granite.

The round tower dominates the monastic city. Although it is built at the bottom of the valley, it can be seen by travellers approaching from every direction. It is about 30 metres high, and a watchman at the top could spot attackers advancing from either end of the valley, or over the mountains. At the top, four windows face the compass points; beneath were six floors, four of them each lit by a tiny window. Since a monastery served as a sanctuary not only for people but also for goods and cattle, looting was frequent. Glendalough is first recorded as being burnt in 770. Over the next 400 years, annals note its destruction on nineteen occasions. Danes attacked nine times, Irish plunderers once, and three times there were accidental fires.

The finest abbot after Kevin was Laurence O'Toole (1123–80), who was born into a ruling family west of the Wicklow Mountains. As a boy, he was handed over as a resident hostage to the King of Ferns. This was a normal practice whereby a greater king secured the loyalty of a lesser one. The King of Ferns treated Laurence harshly, and when his father intervened, Laurence was placed in the custody of the Bishop of

Glendalough. He became attracted to the monastic life, and entered the community; by the age of thirty, he was already its abbot. Soon after his appointment, there was a severe famine. He used the monastery's treasures and some of his own property to feed the poor and to build churches; there was much building at Glendalough during this time. After nine years he became Archbishop of Dublin and left Glendalough, but he returned for periods of solitude to Kevin's Desert beside the Upper Lake.

During the twelfth-century reforms of the Irish Church, Glendalough was handed over to a group of Augustinian canons, but it was destroyed several times, and finally suppressed in the sixteenth century. Pilgrims continued to visit the site, especially to celebrate St Kevin's feast day. In 1873, William Wilde wrote that as a youth he had often attended the celebration: great crowds of people camped among the ruins. Before dawn there was a procession up the Glendasan river with sick children, to dip them into a pool named Kevin's Keeve. This was later adapted for a saw mill. Stone crosses at various points in the valley may mark stations on the pilgrims' route. The procession ended beside the Upper Lake, in Kevin's Desert.[5] There is now a small retreat centre beside the road above the monastic city, and there are plans to construct hermitages where, once again, people can come to experience the solitude and beauty of the valley.

CHAPTER SIX

BRENDAN THE NAVIGATOR

rendan (d. *c.* 575) was a monk of Munster origin. His family name, moccu Altai, indicates that he belonged to the Alltraige, a tribe who lived in the region of north Kerry. Brendan was said to have been tutored by Bishop Erc of Kerry, and to have been one of the 'twelve apostles' who followed the leadership of Finnian of Clonard (see Chapter Seven). We know little about Brendan, but he seems to have been one of many monks who chose the ocean as a focus for their monastic exile. Writing in the seventh century, Adomnán says that Brendan visited Columba on the island of Hinba, off the Scottish west coast. Throughout medieval times, Brendan was a patron of sailors, and churches in a number of coastal settlements are named after him.[1]

Brendan's cathedral at Ardfert is built in his own tribal territory, 3 miles from the Kerry coast. The discovery of an ogham-inscribed stone and some graves beneath the eleventh-century cathedral indicate that this was an early monastic site. Ardfert means 'height of the graves', and much of north Kerry is visible from the low ridge on which the monastery was built. A stone church on the site was damaged by lightning in 1046; some of its masonry survives in the cathedral's north wall. A round tower was built at around this time; it collapsed in 1776, and only its base remains.

In the twelfth century, Ardfert was declared a diocese. Some time after 1130, a fine Romanesque cathedral was built, with an imposing west doorway modelled on Cormac's Chapel at Cashel. The rest of the cathedral was later rebuilt. There are two smaller churches within the monastic enclosure; the earliest, named Temple na Hoe (or 'church of the Virgin'), was built in the twelfth century. The photograph overleaf illustrates its steeply pitched roof. Unusually, columns with carved capitals decorate its outer corners. A second church, Temple na Griffin, was built beside it in the fifteenth century.

Brendan's monastery of Clonfert is some 95 miles north-east of Ardfert. It lies 2 miles west of the River Shannon, and only six miles south of Clonmacnoise on the opposite bank (see Chapter Four). The name Clonfert means 'water meadow of the graves', and well describes the fertile low-lying site where people brought their dead for burial alongside the monks. Brendan is believed to have founded Clonfert in

28. Temple na Hoe, Ardfert.

about 558, about 20 years before his death. It was pillaged by Danes who sailed up the Shannon from Limerick and burned the monastery in 1016, 1164 and 1179.

The earliest surviving feature of the monastery is a cruciform walk of yew trees perhaps dating from the tenth century. Inside the cathedral, a door in the north wall of the chancel leads into an early sacristy, in which marks of the wattle roofing can be seen in the low plastered ceiling. Clonfert's magnificent west doorway is seen in the photograph opposite. It is perhaps the finest example of twelfth-century Irish Romanesque carving. The door is surrounded by a pediment decorated with carved men's heads, set within a geometric design. Some heads are old and bearded, while others are young and clean-shaven. It recalls the ancient Celtic head-cult, in which the entrance to a chieftain's stronghold might be decorated with the potent heads of ancestors or foes.

The first stage of *The Voyage of St Brendan*, one of the most popular stories in medieval times, is set in Clonfert. According to the story, which was written in about 780, Brendan was living at Clonfert as the abbot of a community of about three thousand brothers, when he was visited by a monk named Barrind. This traveller had visited the island monastery of St Mernóc, near Slieve League in Donegal. Barrind described Mernóc's monastery as an ideal community in which monks lived in scattered dwellings, but gathered to celebrate the Eucharist like the monks of the Near Eastern deserts. They ate

29. The west doorway, Clonfert.

frugally and kept the great silence each night. While Barrind was staying with Mernóc, he was told about the Promised Land of the Saints. Barrind had set sail through thick fog and reached the heavenly Jerusalem, full of precious stones, with all its plants in flower and a river flowing across it from east to west. Barrind describes his experience using words taken from chapters 21–2 of the Book of Revelation at the end of the New Testament. Barrind added that he had returned home after a year.

In chapter 2 of the *Navigatio* (or 'Voyage'), after hearing Barrind's story, Brendan chooses fourteen monks from his own community in Clonfert and tells them that he too wishes to sail to the Promised Land of the Saints.[2] They eagerly volunteer to accompany him, and Brendan returns to his native Kerry in order to set out. As a good monk, he avoids visiting his parents, in obedience to Christ's challenge of turning one's back on father and mother for the sake of the gospel.[3] Instead, Brendan and his monks pitch their tent beside a narrow creek under a mountain named Brendan's Seat. This was probably Brandon Creek, at the foot of Brandon Mountain, at the north-west end of the Dingle peninsula. Here Brendan built a wooden-framed boat covered with oxhides. In the boat he and his fellow-monks put a mast and a sail, with supplies of food and water for forty days.

In Christian iconography, a boat symbolises the Church, in which we sail safely across life's stormy sea to heaven, much as Noah saved a remnant of the created world from drowning, and brought them safely to a new land lit by the rainbow of God's promise.[4] In Christian art, a ship's wooden mast symbolised the cross of Christ, raised aloft to speed the journey to our heavenly homeland.[5] For Celtic monks, curraghs of animal hides stretched over wooden ribs represented their human flesh bound to the wood of the cross. Monks wandered through the desert of the ocean in their frail skin crafts as true disciples of Christ. They could imitate the followers of Jesus in the storm-tossed boat who cried: 'Lord, save us, or we perish!'[6]

In the *Navigatio*, Brendan and his monks set sail towards the Promised Land and wander the ocean for seven years. The story is an allegory of monastic life with its annual cycle of labour and worship: they sail round in circles, and celebrate the great festivals in the same places each year. A monastic steward appears at intervals with provisions for Brendan's monks; he explains that each year they will spend Holy Thursday on an island of sheep and celebrate Easter on the back of a whale. We remember that the prophet Jonah spent three days in the belly of a whale before being spewed out to safety, and that Jesus used the story to symbolise his resurrection. They will spend from Easter to Pentecost in a paradise of birds, and Christmas in the monastery of St Ailbe. Each day is punctuated by the monastic liturgy: in their island paradise, the birds sing hymns and chant vespers and the other liturgical offices.[7]

When the unknown author of the *Navigatio* described an island of sheep and a paradise of birds, he drew his imagery from real nautical expeditions. A monk named Dicuil, who left Iona around 810 for the imperial court at Aachen, wrote a *Book of the Measurement of the Earth* fifteen years later. In the treatise, he described hermits who sailed from Ireland to settle on small islands, before the Norsemen laid them waste. Dicuil wrote that the islands were filled with countless sheep and very many different sorts of sea-birds. He added: 'I have never found these islands mentioned in the authorities.'

These are likely to be the Faroes, past which monks sailed in order to find what lay to the far north: an island which they named Thule, in a frozen sea, where the sun never set. Geographically, this was Iceland, but Thule also symbolised the Promised Land, the heavenly Jerusalem which has no need of sun or moon, since 'the glory of God is its light'.[8] The far north was understood to be the edge of the world, a mystical place where space and time slowed down, or even stopped. The journey to the

Opposite: 30. Two curraghs moored in Brandon Creek.

Promised Land was a dangerous one, in which each monk struggled with inner and outer demons. The reader of the *Navigatio* is invited into this redemptive journey, with some urgency, for Irish monks believed that the end of the world would come soon; the great Old Testament figures, Enoch and Elijah, would fight the antichrist, then all would die and rise to judgement. Reading the story, we who are not monks should be vigilant, for we know not the day nor the hour.[9]

The *Navigatio* is a monastic romance about God's love for humankind, in its struggle to attain the Promised Land of heaven. Brendan's voyage is our own; like the sailor monks, we await the adventure which is destined for each of us. The author warns us not to initiate the perilous journey, but to await it. When Brendan was about to set sail, three monks came down to the beach and begged to be taken aboard. Brendan agreed, but foretold that two of them would meet a hideous fate, while the third would not return home. For Celtic monks, the virtue of stability did not mean staying in one place, but staying under the authority of one's abbot. The three monks lacked this virtue, and so were weak before the siren voices of temptation. In the photograph, a fifteenth-century mermaid on the chancel arch of Clonfert Cathedral lures unwary monks to destruction as she combs her long, sensuous hair, resting a mirror on her naked body.

31. Mermaid on the chancel arch, Clonfert.

Like all good novels, Brendan's *Navigatio* contains a wealth of observed detail. The volcanoes of southern Iceland are described as a dangerous place where the monks were pelted with hot rocks. Islanders emerged from their forge and hurled great lumps of slag at the defence-less curragh. The whole island seemed on fire; the sea boiled as the molten lava broke its surface. Icebergs become pillars of crystal floating in the sea. The author describes how Brendan saw an enormous column of bright crystal and sailed towards it for three days, his boat enmeshed in silver pack-ice that was harder than marble. The water was clear as glass; even in the iceberg's shadow, the monks could feel the sun's heat. Eventually, like Barrind before him, Brendan reaches the Promised Land. Yet since this is a story of finite monastic life, Brendan is told to return home with some of the heavenly fruit and precious stones, since his last days are near. He returns to his own community, who receive him joyfully. He warns them of his approaching death, receives the sacraments and dies among his brother monks.

Towering above Brandon Creek, Brandon Mountain became a centre for pilgrimage, perhaps as early as the eighth century. At the mountain peak are remains of cells, a chapel and a holy well. Each July, reviving an earlier tradition, pilgrims climb the mountain to visit the shrine at its summit. The western end of the Dingle peninsula became a sacred landscape honouring Brendan. Over four hundred beehive-shaped stone huts are found here, perhaps built as shelters for pilgrims. There are also numerous churches, ogham-inscribed stones and pillars decorated with crosses. A 'Saints' Road' led from Ventry Harbour on the south side of the peninsula to the summit of Brandon Mountain. Pilgrims evidently arrived by sea before walking the 12-mile route that led up the mountain.[10]

Overlooking Smerwick Harbour, a mile from the Saints' Road, is Gallarus Oratory, situated within a small monastic enclosure. Its name means 'curious house', and its shape has been compared with an upturned boat. Like the beehive huts, it is constructed with unmortared stones, each layer set further inwards, to form a curved roof. The 'curious house' is a small rectangular chapel, the most complete of its kind,

32. Gallarus Oratory, Dingle Peninsula.

with its nine ridge- stones intact. Often a corbelled roof of this design collapses in the middle, its weakest point, unless its masons were exceptionally skilled. Such chapels are almost all found in County Kerry. Gallarus Oratory has a low doorway at its western end, with two large lintel stones. A wooden or leather door hung from two projecting stones inside the chapel. At its eastern end, a small circular window splays inwards, to shed morning light on the missal, for the priest to celebrate Eucharist. We can imagine eager, if weary, pilgrims gathered outside to receive the sacrament, before starting their climb up Brandon Mountain.

CHAPTER SEVEN

MORE IRISH SAINTS

CIARÁN OF SAIGHIR

Ciarán of Saighir was an early Irish bishop who worked in southern Ireland before the arrival of Patrick. He was born in west Cork near Cape Clear, at the southernmost tip of Ireland; a ruined church and well are dedicated to Ciarán on Clear Island. He lived a century before his namesake, Ciarán of Clonmacnoise (see Chapter Four). As a young man he went to Europe, where he was baptised and ordained a priest. He returned to his native Ossory, and settled at Saighir in County Offaly, first as a hermit and later as abbot of a large monastery. Saighir is now the small settlement of Seirkieran, 7 miles north of Roscrea and 40 miles north-east of Limerick. Ciarán's monastery is set in rolling hills, with panoramic views in several directions.

His *Life* relates how Ciarán tamed a fierce but frightened wild boar that helped him to collect materials with which to build a church. The author adds: 'This boar was the first disciple, as it were a monk of St Ciarán, in that place.' A wild boar often features in the story of a Celtic monk's chief foundation. Swineherds worked on the edge of settlements, where their pigs could forage in the forest or in the wilderness, where a monk could find a 'desert place', in order to seek God. As he wandered, looking for the place where he would live and die, which would become the place of his resurrection, the appearance of a wild boar came to symbolise God's approval of the site. Readers familiar with the classics would remember that a huge white sow showed Ascanius where to found the great city of Alba Longa. The boar was also an ancient Celtic symbol of power, and was portrayed on regalia, cauldrons and rock carvings.

Ciarán's *Life* also relates how he decreed that the fire in his monastery must not go out. When it was allowed to do so, and the monks could no longer cook or warm themselves, Ciarán prayed and the fire lit itself again.[1] The communal hearth was a

33. Base of a high cross, Seirkieran, visited for healing.

central feature of ancient rural communities, and was held to be holy. In monasteries, the fire lit on Easter night might be kept alive throughout the following year. In a number of saints' *Lives*, fire is rekindled at their prayers, to demonstrate God's power. Christian readers would recall that the great prophet Elijah kindled fire through his prayer, after the prophets of Baal had failed to do so.[2]

Ciarán's monastery became the seat of the bishops of Ossory, and the burial place of its kings. It was plundered many times, and later became an Augustinian priory. The walled monastic compound covers 10 acres. There are a few remains of the Celtic monastery: the stump of a round tower, an early grave slab and the base of a high cross. The water which collects in its socket is believed to cure warts. Ciarán is a much loved saint and on his feast day, 5 March, pilgrims flock to Seirkieran. South of the monastery, beside the R421, a signed track leads to Ciarán's well pool. Nearby is Ciarán's Bush: a hawthorn tree to which clouties are tied, as prayers for healing. The aged bush looks strangely out of place on its grassy island, with cars driving past on either side.

FINNIAN OF CLONARD

The large and famous monastery of Clonard, 34 miles west of Dublin, was founded by Finnian (d. *c.* 549). His tenth-century *Life*, preserved in the *Book of Lismore*, relates that he was born and educated in County Carlow in south-east Ireland, where he made his first three foundations. Finnian then travelled to south Wales, where he spent time in the great Welsh monasteries. He returned to Ireland and established two more communities before settling at Clonard, in County Meath. This was a central location, only 30 miles from the east coast, so it was easy for monks to reach Clonard from mainland Britain and Europe. The settlement was in fertile farmland beside the River Boyne; cows grazing the site today are a reminder that the rich pasture could support a large community. Finnian's *Life* claims that three thousand monks studied at Clonard; so great was Finnian's reputation that he was nicknamed 'Teacher of the saints of Ireland'.When men left Clonard, they took with them a gospel book, a crozier or a reliquary, as they set out to establish their own communities.

34. Clonard: carving of Finnian on the font.

Twelve leading Irish monks were known as Finnian's 'Twelve Apostles'. Among them were Ciarán of Clonmacnoise and Kevin of Glendalough (see Chapters Four and Five), Brendan and Columba (see Chapters Six and Seventeen). Several of Finnian's 'apostles' had died before his lifetime, or had not yet been born, but the list indicates Clonard's considerable influence. There have been sample excavations at the extensive monastic site, but few remains have been uncovered. Down a grassy track, a modern church stands within the ancient graveyard. Set in the ground near the church porch is a large rectangular stone container for water from the monastery. Its brackish water was said to cause death to animals but to cure warts. Another artefact that has survived is an elaborate bucket, only 2.5 centimetres tall. It is bound with a bronze hoop, and its handle clasps are decorated with fine carving and precious stones. It was perhaps used to contain holy water.

The *Penitential of Finnian* was probably written at Clonard. This is a manual of punishments for crimes, based partly on Irish and Welsh sources, and also on the writings of Jerome and Cassian. Much of it, however, is original. It is the oldest of the Irish penitentials, which made an important contribution to the Church's understanding of pastoral care.[3] Finnian died of plague; his relics were enshrined at Clonard until the monastery was destroyed in 887. It was rebuilt in the twelfth century, and its monks adopted the Augustinian rule. A magnificent fifteenth-century font survives from the abbey. It can be seen in the modern Catholic church beside the busy N6 in Clonard village. Lively scenes are carved on its panels: Joseph leads a donkey by the halter as the Holy Family flees to Egypt, and a smiling Bishop Finnian raises his hand in blessing, while an angel beside him holds a gospel book (see previous page).

COLMAN OF KILMACDUAGH

There were some three hundred Celtic saints named Colmán, a word meaning 'little dove'. Colmán of Kilmacduagh (d. *c.* 632) was born in the mid-sixth century. He became a monk on Aran Island, off Ireland's north-west coast, and then returned south to County Clare, where he settled in the Burren Hills, and was unwillingly consecrated a bishop. He lived here with a disciple, on an austere diet of vegetables and water. Colmán later founded the monastery of Kilmacduagh on land given to him by his kinsman, Guaire the Generous, King of Connaght. Guaire lived in the nearby town of Gort, and provided the workmen and materials to build Colmán's monastery. Legends about Colmán tell how a cockerel used to wake him in time for the night office, a mouse prevented him from going to sleep during his silent vigil afterwards, and a fly kept the place in his prayer book. Part of Colmán's crozier is in Dublin, in the National Museum of Ireland.

35. Round tower, Kilmacduagh.

Kilmacduagh, 17 miles south of Galway, is one of the finest Irish monastic sites, set in green meadows near the shore of a lough, with the Burren Hills on the horizon. The cathedral is the largest building in the monastic enclosure: it occupies the site of a rectangular seventh-century church. Its west end, with its lintelled doorway, roof corbels and steeply pitched gable, was probably built before the eleventh century.[4] Colmán was said to be buried in a shrine outside the cathedral. Nearby, the ruined church of St John the Baptist dates from the tenth century. Remains of Our Lady's church stand beside the road that was driven through the site in the eighteenth century. Next to St John's church, the Glebe House was the later bishops' residence. From an upstairs oriel window, the bishop used to bless pilgrims who gathered here on Colmán's feast day, 29 October.[5]

The most striking feature of the site is a tenth-century round tower, 30 metres high. It is the tallest in Ireland, and leans 0.6 metres out of perpendicular. This is probably because it lacks deep foundations: it was built on soft earth, on the site of an early Christian burial ground. When the tower was restored in the late nineteenth century, skeletons were found lying oriented east to west beneath the centre of the tower and below its walls. The tower had seven timber floors, where many people could take refuge. The lowest portion of the tower was found to be filled with large and small stones; above this, human bones found in a deposit of ash provided evidence of a disastrous fire. Copper fragments suggested that monks had taken refuge in the tower, taking their precious church vessels with them.[6] Viking raiders plundered the site in the tenth century, and the monastery was destroyed by Normans in the thirteenth. It was restored by the local chieftain and by Augustinian canons; its cemetery continues to be used by families from the surrounding area.

FECHÍN OF FORE

Fechín was a holy man from Sligo who travelled widely in Ireland. His first foundation was at Fore in Westmeath, and he later established other communities including one at Cong beside Lough Corrib, from which a fine metal cross survives. Fechín also founded monasteries on a couple of islands. The earliest manuscript of his *Life* comes

36. Entrance to Fechín's church, Fore.

from his island settlement of Ard Oilean, off the coast of Connemara. There are monastic ruins at most of Fechín's foundations, a few dating from his lifetime. Fechín died of the Yellow Plague in the 660s. His cult was taken by his followers to Scotland, where the monastery of St Vigeans at Arbroath near the Fife coast is named after him. An impressive collection of Pictish grave slabs survives at the monastery.

Fore, 20 miles west of Navan, is an interesting site. In the tenth century a simple rectangular church was built on the hillside here. Its west doorway can be seen in the photograph: on its giant lintel is a carved cross within a circular design. A small graveyard surrounds the church. The monastery was a bishopric until the twelfth century, when the Normans built a large Benedictine abbey in the valley below, and life probably ended at Fechín's foundation. Between the two sites, a ruined mill is said to be on the site of one built by Fechín. It is fed by underground streams from Lough Lene, a mile away, on the far side of the mountain. The rivulets emerge from the hillside and flow into a triangular millpond before continuing through the ruined mill.

Between the mill and the Benedictine abbey, beneath an ancient ash tree, is Fechín's holy well. It is a triangular structure, its walls formed by three great stone slabs; it is named Doaghfeighín, or Fechín's Vat. It is now dry, but formerly contained water in which Fechín was said to have knelt in prayer. Delicate children were immersed in the water to be cured through Fechín's intercession. Gnarled roots of the ash tree are now entwined with the stones of Fechín's Vat. Clouties are tied to the tree, as mute prayers for healing.

MANCHÁN

Twelve miles east of the great monastery of Clonmacnoise (see Chapter Four), on a small island rising out of the bog, a monk named Manchán established a hermitage in the early seventh century. Lemanaghan means 'Manchán's grey place'. When Manchán's patron, Diarmuid, King of Ireland, marched to battle against Guaire, King of Connacht, in 645, he is said to have passed through Clonmacnoise, where the congregation prayed to St Ciarán for his safe return. Diarmuid won the battle, and gave the people 'Manchán's grey place' in memory of his victory. Manchán settled here with his mother Mella; a small stone oratory on the site is known as her cell. Both Manchán and Diarmuid died in the great plague of 664–6.

The former island in the bog is now a low mound on which are the remains of two Romanesque churches and six early grave slabs. At the lower end of the site, a short track leads to Manchán's well, which is approached down a flight of stone steps. Near the well is an ancient ash tree with knotted roots and branches, to which local people tie clouties. Beside the well is a bullaun stone, a feature of many early monastic sites: a

37. Manchán's shrine, Lemanaghan.

large stone with a cavity containing water. It may have been used for washing, or perhaps its water was blessed and used in worship.

Part of an eleventh-century crozier was found in the bog, and Manchán's shrine was also recovered: it is now displayed in the nearby Catholic church at Boher. The shrine was made around 1130; it contains a number of bones, believed to be Manchán's. It is constructed of yew wood in the shape of a gabled box 48 centimetres high. With its cast gilt bronze and red and yellow fittings, its lavish decoration resembles that of the Cross of Cong, fashioned in about 1123. The processional cross from Cong is very different in shape, however, carved out of oak and designed to encase a relic of the Cross of Christ at its centre.

Manchán's shrine is ornamented on either side with an elaborate metal cross, each having five prominent bosses. Around the two crosses stood fifty elongated human figures, eleven of which have survived. There are interwoven beasts and serpents at the corners and at each end of the shrine, carved in an Irish version of a late Scandinavian style. During processions, the shrine was carried on a pair of wooden poles, threaded through rings mounted at each corner. This is the largest and most magnificent shrine to have been found in Ireland.

MOLING

The cult of Moling (d. 697) was early and widespread. Moling came from a noble Leinster family and became a monk at Glendalough (see Chapter Five). He later founded his own monastery at St Mullins, beside the River Barrow in County Carlow. The river winds between high wooded banks, as it flows south towards Waterford Harbour. Moling is said to have established a ferry across the River Barrow, it is still in existence. Moling lived for a time in a hermitage near St Mullins. He later became bishop of Ferns, which lies to the east, over the Blackstairs Mountains. Here he is said to have helped the people by obtaining the remission of a heavy tribute of oxen to the local king.

38. Chapel at St Mullins well.

In about 1160, Moling's monastery was annexed to the abbey of Augustinian canons at Ferns. The canons were responsible for building the six medieval churches, now in ruins, that dominate St Mullins; they may also have built St Moling's Mill. However, there are earlier remains: the base of a round tower, a small chapel, 2.5 metres long, and the remains of a high cross carved in granite in the ninth or tenth century, with a Crucifixion scene. On the opposite bank of the river is Moling's holy well. The water passes through a large pool into a well chapel, before flowing down to the River Barrow.

There is a small pocket gospel book in Trinity College, Dublin, named the *Book of Mulling*; it is encased in an elaborate shrine of bronze with silver plates, and it was probably written in the ninth century, copied from a manuscript written by Moling. It contains the gospels, a Mass for the Sick and a simplified plan of the monastery at St Mullins, whose boundary wall is indicated by two concentric circles. Outside the enclosure, eight crosses commemorate Old Testament prophets and the four evangelists. One dedicated to the Holy Spirit was erected on or beside the boundary wall, and three more, possibly decorated with scenes from the scriptures, stood inside the compound. It is one of these three that survives at the site. The plan suggests that monasteries were adorned with far more crosses than have survived, and the drawing provides unexpected evidence that crosses were erected outside the boundary wall of a monastic enclosure as well as within it. The fact that no buildings are marked on the plan, while the locations of the crosses are carefully plotted, also indicates that, symbolically at least, high crosses were a significant feature of Irish monastic life.

PART II

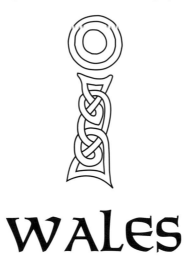

WALES

Map 2: Saints of Wales

CHAPTER EIGHT

DAVID AND HIS MOTHER, NON

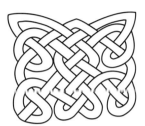

David (d. *c.* 589) worked in south-west Wales, in what is now Pembrokeshire. Most of our knowledge about him comes from a *Life of David* written by Rhigyfarch in about 1095. The author came from a distinguished family of scholarly monks and clerics who contributed to Welsh life and learning in Norman times. Rhigyfarch's father had been bishop of St David's for 10 years, and attended a meeting between William the Conqueror and two Welsh princes in 1081 at this remote cathedral. The Welsh chieftains probably appealed to William to uphold the independence of the Welsh Church against the increasing power of Rome. Rhigyfarch may have written his *Life of David* for this occasion, as a statement about the authority of their Church and the holiness of its founder.[1] Rhigyfarch tells us that David's father was Sant, King of Ceredigion, and his mother, from the neighbouring kingdom of Dyfed, was called Non. It was seen as fitting that David's parents should be named Sant (from the Latin word *sanctus* or 'holy') and Non, meaning 'nun'.

Non's medieval chapel stands on Celtic foundations, on a clifftop in St Non's Bay, a mile south of St David's Cathedral. Much of the chapel was demolished in 1810; nearby farmers used the stone to repair their field boundaries.[2] This is an early site: nineteenth-century excavations revealed slab-lined or 'cist' graves, probably dating from between the seventh and ninth centuries, to the east and south of the chapel. Inside, a gravestone carved with a simple ringed cross comes from the same period. In the foreground of the photograph overleaf is a giant boulder, part of a Bronze Age stone circle within which Non's chapel was built. Tradition relates that here she gave birth to her son: a storm was raging, but inside the stone circle it was calm and sunny!

St Non's chapel is one of eight medieval oratories dotted around the headlands of St David's peninsula, each within a few miles of the cathedral. Pilgrims travelled here by sea from north Wales, southern Ireland, Cornwall and Brittany. They climbed up from the shore below to give thanks for their safe arrival, for their small boats were at the mercy of winds, tides and the many currents around the coast. Navigators could not always choose where to land, but there are small harbours near each chapel, with pathways leading to St David's.[3]

39. Bronze Age standing stone, St Non's Bay.

Close to St Non's chapel is her holy well. This is one of the chief healing wells of Wales; it was famous for curing eye diseases. Holy wells were often visited for eye ailments because a spring was considered to be an eye upon the face of mother earth. In the early eighteenth century, Browne Willis wrote: 'There is a fine well . . . covered with a stone roof and enclosed within a wall, with benches to sit upon round the well. Some old, simple people go still to visit this saint. . . . especially upon St Nun's day (2 March), which they keep holy and offer pins, pebbles etc at this well.'[4]

A century later, the well was still popular, as Fenton reported: 'The fame this consecrated spring had obtained is incredible, and still it is resorted to for many complaints. In my infancy . . . I was often dipped in it, and offerings, however trifling, even a farthing or a pin, were made after each ablution, and the bottom of the well shone with votive brass.'[5] In the field leading to the chapel, there was a house for the well's caretaker. The well-house was restored in 1951.

David was raised at Henfynyw, just south of Aberaeron, on the coast road to Aberystwyth. Here a church stands on a cliff overlooking the sea beside a steep-sided valley where boats could land. It was known as a place of learning, under the

40. St Non's well, St Non's Bay.

leadership of a bishop named Guistilianus. There was a cemetery here, for part of a large pillar stone commemorates a Christian called Tigeir(nacus). It was erected between the seventh and the ninth century. An ancient well stood at the northern corner of the churchyard.[6] In summer, the cemetery surrounding the church is bright with orange fox-and-cubs and other wild flowers.

David rose to a position of leadership during the Synod of Brefi (*c.* 545), which appears to have been a religious tribal gathering to refute the heretical teachings of Pelagius. This British theologian taught that people could reach heaven by their own efforts, without the help of God's grace. His emphasis on personal responsibility appealed to British tribal chieftains, with their strong sense of self-reliance. The gathering took place at what is now Llanddewi Brefi (or 'David's church beside the River Brefi'). The settlement was a natural place to assemble: three Roman roads converge nearby, and continued in use long after the Romans departed, although by the mid-sixth century they were probably becoming overgrown.

At the synod, no one could make their voice heard over such a large crowd. David was a clear, convincing speaker, and was brought from nearby to address the gathering. When Rhigyfarch relates this detail, Welsh readers would recall that a victorious bard could silence his opponents, just as only David could quieten the crowd and convince them of the errors of Pelagius.[7] From this time onwards, David began to be seen as a tribal bishop. He wore rough clothes and carried a large branch, rather than a crozier. He apparently went about bareheaded and barefoot, carrying a bell which he named *bangu*, or 'dear, loud one'. Inside Llanddewi Brefi church there is a fine collection of early gravestones; that in the photograph dates from between the seventh and the ninth centuries. Set into the outer wall of the church are two fragments of an inscription dating from the fifth, sixth or seventh century which may

41. Celtic gravestone, Llanddewi Brefi.

be the first surviving reference to David. The antiquarian Edward Lhuyd examined the complete stone, and concluded in 1722 that it read: 'Here lies Idnert, the son of Jacob, who was killed while defending the church of holy David from pillage.'[8]

David travelled south-west along the coast to a headland where he established a monastery at what is now St David's. He chose a site in the narrow valley of the River Alun, hidden from pirates by a bend in the river. Here he built a small church of mud and timber, and huts for monks. A section of Rhigyfarch's *Life of David* draws on an early source and relates how the monks grew their food, working hard with mattocks, hoes and axes. They ploughed the fields themselves, instead of using oxen, and spent the rest of the day reading, writing and praying. In the evening they gathered in the church for vespers, and then prayed silently until night fell. Only then would they eat together: a simple meal of 'bread and herbs, seasoned with salt', eaten in moderation and washed down with

ale. David himself lived on bread, vegetables and water.[9] In the same way, the Irish monk Brendan (see Chapter Six) was described as eating no meat. Later, a movement of monks who called themselves Céli Dé (or 'Servants of God') urged a return to a stricter lifestyle and a more austere diet. The monastery of St David's may have been influenced by the Irish Céli Dé.[10]

After their frugal meal, the monks returned to chapel to pray for another few hours. After a short night's sleep, they woke at cock-crow to sing matins and to 'spend the rest of the night until morning without sleep'. There was little emphasis on study, in contrast to the value placed on learning in the monasteries of south-east Wales. Anyone seeking to join the community was to be kept waiting outside the door for ten days, to test his desire for monastic life. The candidate was then welcomed by the doorkeeper, and put to work alongside the monks for many months, 'until the natural stubbornness of his heart was broken'. When the abbot judged that he was well prepared, the novice was eventually invited to join the community.[11] The pattern of life in David's monastery was unusually severe; it was designed to imitate that of monks in the Near Eastern deserts.

David's bones are preserved in an oak casket, together with those of a hermit named Justinian, who lived on the island of Ramsey, west of St David's. According to his *Life*, Justinian came from a noble Breton family, but was murdered in his island home by his servants. A chapel and a holy well are dedicated to him in St Justinian's Bay on the mainland, overlooking Ramsey. Justinian was said to have been a friend of David, and had a widespread and ancient cult. The casket containing the relics of the two monks is modern, but in medieval times, pilgrims flocked to David's shrine in the cathedral sanctuary; its thirteenth-century stonework can still be seen.

Church dedications suggest that early followers of David may have worked in Cornwall and Brittany. There are nine ancient churches named after David in Cornwall, including that of Davidstow, on the edge of Bodmin Moor (see map 4). This bleak moorland

42. Reliquary in St David's Cathedral.

village is 12 miles west of Launceston. Its former name was Dewstow: David's name is *Dewi Sant* in Welsh. There are some fine thirteenth-century carved bench ends in the church, including a rare depiction of a minstrel blowing the Cornish bagpipes. These instruments were played in Celtic times. In a field east of the church, clearly signed from the road, lies St David's holy well. The rectangular pool is protected by a modern stone well-house. Its water is so pure that it is used by the local creamery, whose mild Davidstow cheese is widely sold.

43. A minstrel plays the Cornish bagpipes, Davidstow.

Seven miles south-east of Davidstow, the settlement of Altarnun ('Non's altar') is dedicated to David's mother. She is honoured with a fine church here beside a fast-flowing stream in a valley. A tall Celtic cross in the churchyard may date from this time. In a field above the church, Non's holy well feeds a bowssening pool. This is a pond into which deranged people were tumbled, in a primitive form of shock therapy. They were then taken down to the church, where Masses were sung for their recovery.[12]

Non may also be remembered in south-east Cornwall at Pelynt, 4 miles west of Looe (see map 4). Its name comes from *plou Nent*, which means 'parish of Non'. Pelynt is the only example of a Cornish church name that incorporates the word *plou*, although it is often found in Brittany.[13] Her holy well is a mile down the valley in Hobb Park, where a spring emerges from the hillside. Although restored, the well-house retains its original shape, with a curved roof, a stone lintel, and walls of flat, unmortared stones. On either side of the entrance is a stone bench where pilgrims could sit and pray.

Inside the well-house, water trickles into a heavy bowl of pink granite, incised with wheel crosses; it dates from Celtic times. Earlier this century, the outline of a mound and wall could still be traced above the well: this may have been a chapel.[14] There is a third holy well dedicated to Non at St Mawgan-in-Pydar near the north Cornish coast, 5 miles north-east of Newquay. In Brittany, Non is sometimes commemorated as a male companion of David. Non died in western Brittany, and is buried at Dirinon, 10 miles east of Brest.

Opposite: 44. Non's well, Pelynt.

CHAPTER NINE

CADOC AND THE GREAT SOUTHERN MONASTERIES

Before Christianity reached Ireland, there were probably Christians in Wales who arrived with the Roman army and administration. Inscriptions on their tombstones suggest that they were educated people, who spoke Latin rather than Welsh. In the fifth and sixth centuries, Christians travelled from Gaul to Wales, where gravestones are inscribed in a style found in Gaul. By this time, monasteries were well established in Gaul, and immigrants brought with them an experience of monastic life. By the early sixth century there were a number of Welsh communities, and the monastic tradition spread rapidly. By the twelfth century there were thirty-six communities in south-east Wales. As in Ireland, early Welsh monasteries included both monks and non-monastic priests. They were presided over by an abbot, who was often a bishop. He was normally married, and leadership was handed down through the family.[1]

Cadoc was a leading figure among the monks of south Wales in the early sixth century. We know little about him, because the two earliest biographies of Cadoc, written 500 years after his death, are unreliable collections of legends. Cadoc was of noble birth: his father, to whom Newport Cathedral is dedicated, was a prince of Gwent in south-east Wales. Cadoc's mother, Gwladys, was a daughter of Brychan, the ruler of Brecon, which lies to the north-east of Gwent. Brychan was a chieftain whose twenty-four sons and daughters helped to spread Christianity in south Wales. His family will be described more fully in Chapter Twenty. Cadoc's father was said to have been reckless and lawless, while his mother Gwladys was devout.

Cadoc was nicknamed 'the Wise'. There is a cluster of churches dedicated to him in the upper Usk valley, centred on Llangattock-nigh-Usk (church of Cadoc near the Usk) in his father's territory, 5 miles north-west of Abergavenny. Cadoc had been baptised in the nearby Onneu brook, and he later returned to evangelise the people in the hill-fort across the river.[2] Today sheep graze in Llangattock churchyard, around the squat twelfth-century tower and the Tudor porch. Inside, the church is spacious:

45. Llangattock church.

the photograph above depicts the fourteenth-century arcade which divides the double chancel and nave.

The broad River Usk has carved a valley at the foot of the hill-fort where Cadoc is said to have spent time preaching. The name 'Usk' comes from a Celtic word meaning 'water'. Rivers were an important means of travel in Celtic times, when much of the land was forest, mountain or undrained marsh. Some Roman roads survived, strongly built for troops to march along, but these gradually fell into ruin.

River travel was by coracle: this was a light, circular craft, constructed of hide stretched over a wicker frame. The style of construction and type of wood differed in each locality, depending on the speed of the river and the types of material available. Even today, Welsh coracle men are skilled at using coracles for a range of activities from fishing to dipping sheep and salmon poaching, as well as for transport. We can imagine Celtic monks using them in the same way.

As a youth, Cadoc is said to have studied at Caerwent, 10 miles east of Newport, in a monastery founded by an Irish monk named Tathan. Caerwent was an ancient tribal capital, and was the largest centre of civilian population in Roman Wales. One can still

46. The River Usk below Llangattock.

walk round its impressive walls with their defensive towers. There was a Christian community here in Roman times, and evidence of two house churches has been found. One house was redesigned to include a nave, an eastern apse, a porch and sacristies. In the other house church, a sealed urn contained a pewter bowl with the *chi-rho* symbol for Christ scratched on it, and other vessels that were perhaps used for the meal that followed the Eucharist in the fourth century.

Two hundred years after the Romans withdrew, Tathan built a church near the centre of the ruined Roman town. An ancient yew tree stands in the churchyard (see overleaf). Roman masonry is incorporated into the church walls, and a Saxon font has a Roman column for its base. We know little about Tathan. His later *Life* describes him as the 'Father of all Gwent. He was the defender of the woodland country. . . . He was never angry. . . . Whatever was given to him, he gave to others . . . no one was more generous in the west for receiving guests and giving them hospitality.' Tathan probably died in Caerwent.[3] Cadoc later founded a monastery of his own at Llancarfan, 4 miles north-west of Barry, and a group of monks from Caerwent was said to have joined him.

47. Ancient yew in Caerwent churchyard.

As we have seen, when a monk founded a monastery, it was important that he should discover the place where God wanted him to live. Before selecting his site at Llancarfan, Cadoc and his monks spent the night in prayer, and in the morning a white boar appeared, to indicate where he should begin building. This is a recurring theme in stories of Celtic saints' foundations: the white boar becomes a messenger from God, as we saw in the story of Ciarán of Saighir (Chapter Seven). The pig foundation tales take place in a timeless world of pseudo-history. In the *Life of Cadoc* by Lifris of Llancarfan, a large white boar leaps out from a thicket, frightened by Cadoc's approach. It shows Cadoc where to build a church in honour of the Trinity, with a dormitory and a refectory. However, this is an Anglo-Norman pig, for a dormitory, a refectory and a Trinitarian dedication are features of a Norman monastery rather than a Celtic one.

The name Llancarfan means 'church of the stags', from a legend about Cadoc: when he asked two monks to till the ground near the monastery, they refused, but a pair of stags appeared from the woods and dug the soil with their antlers. There were several great monasteries in the Vale of Glamorgan: that of St Illtud at Llanilltud Fawr (or Llantwit Major in English), only 5 miles west of Llancarfan, and that of St Docco at Llandough, now a northern suburb of Penarth, further to the east. Llancarfan was beside a stream not far from the sea, which has now receded. It may have been an ancient port, safely upstream, hidden from pirates. Like Llanilltud Fawr, it was near the main road through south Wales, and far enough up the Bristol Channel to provide an easy sea-crossing.

Cadoc and Illtud worked among the descendants of Romano-British Christians. The twelfth-century *Life of Cadoc* describes him as coming from an imperial Roman family, loving the works of Virgil and regretting that, as a Christian, he would be unable to meet the pagan poet in heaven! The Celtic monastery at Llancarfan probably lies below the field to the south of the present church; a well in the next field is also associated with the monastery. It was a centre of learning, with a large number of monks. The community was ravaged by the Danes in 988. The present church is medieval; its fine carved oak screen (below) dates from the Perpendicular period.

Besides working in the upper Usk valley, Cadoc spent time further south in Caerleon. Here, where the tidal river was still navigable, the Romans built the legionary fortress of Isca. Troops could assemble here, their supplies easily transported by land or sea. The name Caerleon means 'Camp of the Legions', and Cadoc's church

48. Carved oak screen, Llancarfan.

49. The tidal River Usk at Caerleon.

is near the centre of the ruined fort. Bede tells us that in the third century, two Roman soldiers were arrested at Caerleon and executed for their Christian beliefs. They belonged to the Second Augustan Legion and were named Julius and Aaron.[4] They were buried south-east of the town, across the river, in the Christian portion of the Roman cemetery. In medieval times, a chapel dedicated to Julius and Aaron stood on the site. It lies in the present parish of Christchurch, on the wooded ridge across the river, to the right of the photograph.

When the Romans withdrew in the early fifth century, local dynasties of Welsh chieftains ruled. Cadoc sprang from one of these dynasties, and a number of churches named after him are associated with Roman forts and settlements. Cadoc's church in Caerleon was beside the crossroads at the town centre. Part of a ninth-century high cross survives, decorated with bird-like angels and interlaced patterns. It stood at the crossroads, outside the churchyard. The Roman ruins in Caerleon provided immense supplies of good building stone, and almost all of the town's older buildings utilise recycled Roman material. Incorporated into the fifteenth-century tower of Cadoc's church are red sandstone blocks, orange brick tiles and yellow freestone, all of Roman origin.

Cadoc's church at Caerleon is built over the *principia*, or legionary headquarters, where the imperial standards were kept, and statues of the emperor were venerated. On this site the Christian soldiers, Julius and Aaron, would have refused to pay homage to the deified emperor. Beneath the churchyard, the fine mosaic floor of the

50. Roman labyrinth mosaic, Caerleon. (Reproduced by permission of the National Museum of Wales)

principia was discovered. It depicts a labyrinth; around its border, a stylised tree of life emerges from a vase. The mosaic is now preserved in the museum across the road. We can imagine Julius and Aaron standing within the maze, trapped between life and death, on account of their beliefs.[5]

Not far from the church are the legionary barracks where Julius and Aaron would have slept, and the giant amphitheatre where the soldiers trained. After their arrest, they would have been sent to the civil settlement of Caerwent, 8 miles to the east, to be tried by the judiciary. As Roman citizens, they would not have been subjected to the sadistic indignities of the amphitheatre games at Caerleon; instead, they were probably beheaded, in about AD 304. Ironically, within 10 years the converted Emperor Constantine gave Christians freedom to worship.[6]

According to his twelfth-century *Life*, Cadoc also was martyred, in the late sixth century. While he was celebrating the Eucharist in his old age, in his monastery at Llancarfan, a Saxon warrior entered the church on horseback and pierced him with a lance. Cadoc's followers took his cult north and south. A chapel and holy well were named after him in Harlyn Bay at Cadoc Farm, on the north Cornish coast, while far to the north in Glasgow, Cadoc is honoured in the settlement of Cambuslang, above the River Clyde.

CHAPTER TEN

BEUNO, A MISSIONARY IN NORTH WALES

North Wales was separated from the south by mountains and forests in Celtic times, and so it developed a culture of its own. While David and his followers worked in south Wales, much of the north was evangelised by Beuno. His *Life* survives only in a fourteenth-century Welsh translation of a lost Latin *Life*, made by a hermit at Llanddewi Brefi in Ceredigion. Early churches dedicated to Beuno appear to confirm the outline of the *Life*. Most early Welsh saints of any significance worked in the south; Beuno is one of the few known Celtic monks who lived and worked in north Wales.

Beuno was born of a noble family in mid-Wales in the second half of the sixth century. He was said to have trained for the priesthood in one of the great monasteries of the south, and returned to his father's territory of Powys. His *Life* relates that after his father's death, a local prince gave Beuno the small settlement of Berriew, 5 miles south-west of Welshpool, as a site for his first monastery. Its name (Aber Rhiw in Welsh) indicates that Berriew grew beside the River Rhiw where it flows into the Severn, near the Roman road to Wroxeter. The monolith known as *Maen Beuno* (or 'Beuno's Stone') is shown overleaf; it is a pointed Bronze Age standing stone in Dyffryn Lane, a mile from Beuno's church. This perhaps marked the settlement's holy place and here, according to tradition, Beuno preached to the people, at the beginning of his missionary career.

Beuno appears to have remained in Berriew for some years, until, according to his *Life*, he was frightened by the sight of a Saxon warrior patrolling on the far side of the River Severn. In the face of the advancing English, he decided to move to safety, and travelled north-west through the Berwyn Mountains into the valley of the River Dee. There is a cluster of dedications to Beuno in the Dee valley around Gwyddelwern, 8 miles west of Llangollen. Beuno is said to have founded a community at Gwyddelwern, which lies on a Roman road.[1]

Since *Wyddel* means 'Irishman', the name of the village indicates that it was settled by Irish immigrants. Groups of farming families in search of land for pasture migrated

51. Beuno's stone, Berriew.

from Ireland to Wales during this period. The yew tree at Gwyddelwern pre-dates the church, which is dedicated to Beuno. Beside the road half a mile to the north is the settlement's holy well. Older inhabitants remember this being the sole source of water for the village. People used to bathe in the well, believing in its miraculous powers, and water was taken to the church for baptisms.

A group of churches named after Beuno near the Flint coast suggests that he and his followers continued northwards. Beuno was said to be the uncle of St Winifred and, according to her *Life*, he obtained land from her parents at Holywell, where he built a church. His cell was probably on the site of the present parish church; a well across the road on top of Castle Hill also bears his name.[2] Now submerged beneath brambles, it has been superseded by Winifred's famous well at the foot of the hill, which will be described in the following chapter.

His *Life* recounts that Beuno travelled 50 miles west along the coast to Caernarvon, where he asked the chieftain, Cadwallon, for a site on which to build a church. Cadwallon offered him land that belonged to someone else, after which Beuno cursed him angrily. Cadwallon's cousin, Gwyddaint, then offered Beuno land in his own

52. Celtic yew tree, Gwyddelwern churchyard.

53. Beuno's chapel, Clynnog Fawr.

township of Clynnog, 10 miles further along the coast. Around 616, Beuno established a monastery here, where he spent the last phase of his life. Beuno is said to have died here at the end of Easter week in 642. The small chapel at Clynnog is probably built on the site of Beuno's church, and may have contained his tomb. His influence increased until Clynnog came to rival Bangor in importance.

As late as the eighteenth century, pilgrims came to Beuno's shrine to pray for healing. The settlement became known as Clynnog Fawr (Great Clynnog), and a large church was built alongside Beuno's chapel. A late Celtic sundial stands beside the outer wall of the chapel. This is one of Britain's earliest sundials, and would have been used by monks in their ordered life of work and prayer.[3]

The impressive church beside the chapel was extended just before the Reformation to accommodate the crowds of pilgrims who came here to begin walking the Saints' Way, a route which led along the Lleyn peninsula to Bardsey Island at its tip. Beuno's well is 200 metres south-west of the church, beside the main road. A flight of stone steps leads to a pool of clear water in a square well-house. It supplied water for the monastery, and became a famous healing well.

54. Beuno's church, Pistyll.

Ten miles further along the Saints' Way, in a sheltered hollow by the sea, is Beuno's tiny church at Pistyll. A steep track leads down from the main road to the church. It is set inside an oval Celtic enclosure, and built around the great boulder which was its original cornerstone. Ancient fruit bushes still grow in the churchyard, successors of those once tended by Celtic monks: gooseberry, daneberry and sloes, and also hops and medicinal herbs.[4]

In earlier times, the earthen floor of the church was strewn with rushes and sweet-smelling herbs, and parishioners have revived this tradition. It is freshly strewn three times a year, at Christmas, Easter and Lammas Day in early August. One enters through a Romanesque arch, crossing the threshold, a corruption of 'the rush-hold', since it held the rushes inside the church. Local Celtic craftsmen carved Pistyll's twelfth-century font, with its circular interweaving patterns. The church roof was thatched until the 1850s.

Pistyll is Welsh for 'waterfall', and beside the churchyard, a fast-flowing stream tumbles into a large pool. This was the fishpond of the monastery which once stood on the site of Pistyll Farm, opposite the church. Pilgrims could rest at the monastery, or at nearby farms, and many would sleep in shelters in the hospice field which adjoined some of the churches along the Saints' Way. At Pistyll, pilgrims travelling along the Lleyn peninsula could buy food and fuel from the villagers. They were entitled to ask for shelter, bread and cheese, in return for which the villagers were excused from paying rent to their monastic land-owners.

In the sixth century, Anglesey was the island stronghold of Maelgwyn of Gwynedd, whose name means 'Princely Hound'. He made his headquarters at Aberffraw and established a dynasty which ruled until the early ninth century. In his *History of the Britons*, the monk Gildas described him as 'a great king'. Beuno came to Maelgwyn's court to ask permission to build a church and was granted a plot of land in Aberffraw, where the parish church of St Beuno now stands.

On the edge of the town, beside the medieval bridge over the tidal river, older inhabitants recall the site of Beuno's well. It stood in Malthouse Lane, between the river and the main road, but was destroyed when the road was altered. Another ancient church is dedicated to Beuno at nearby Trefdreath. Beuno travelled to Anglesey not across the Menai Strait but further south, landing in the shallow mud flats of Llanddwyn Island near Newborough. From here, it was only a short journey to Aberffraw.

The *Life of Beuno* describes how he gathered followers to work alongside him. A number of these disciples are honoured in settlements close to those of their

55. Medieval bridge at Aberffraw.

56. Llangwyfan, Anglesey.

master. Two miles west of Beuno's church at Aberffraw is the church of Llangwyfan, on an isolated rock which is connected to the mainland at low tide by a causeway. It is named after a follower of Beuno, Cwyfan. The island is less than an acre in area, and in summer the grass in the raised churchyard is studded with pink thrift and golden birdsfoot trefoil.

The single-chambered medieval church replaced a seventh-century chapel. The Eucharist was celebrated here until the mid-nineteenth century on alternate Sundays, when the tide and the weather allowed. The priest was entitled to demand from the proprietor of Plas Llangwyfan on the mainland a tithe of two eggs, a penny loaf, half a pint of beer and hay for his horse. One can imagine the two men sitting down to their meal, with the horse munching the hay outside.

There are three more churches dedicated to Cwyfan, near to those of Beuno: one at Tudweiliog on the Lleyn peninsula; another at Llangwyfan near Gwyddelwern, and a third at Dyserth, 8 miles west of Holywell. Cwyfan's church at Dyserth is at the foot of a high waterfall. The name Dyserth comes from the Latin word *desertum*, which means 'an empty place'. This is the western equivalent of the Greek term *eremos* or 'hermitage', an ancient monastic word that was used by the monks and nuns who went into the deserts of Syria, Egypt and Palestine in search of a solitary place to pray.

57. Dyserth waterfall.

European pilgrims were impressed by the wisdom and holiness of these desert mothers and fathers, and wished to follow their example. Since there were no deserts in Britain, monks searched for a similar 'empty place' on a rocky headland or small island, or in a remote valley. Scattered across Ireland, Scotland and Wales are places named Dyserth, or Díseart in Irish. Each indicates an 'empty place' where a person could search for God in solitude.

Cwyfan or his unknown follower chose a magnificent location for his 'desert', within sound and sight of the waterfall's spray. The pool at its foot provided water for drinking and washing, and a place in which to immerse candidates for baptism. Watercress, valued as food by Celtic monks, grows thickly in the cold stream flowing past the church. Inside, the remains of two elaborate Celtic crosses indicate that a community continued on the site. Half a mile north-west of the church is Cwyfan's holy well, now dry. Earlier this century, people still fished for trout in the well. Fish in wells were regarded with awe and respect, and were considered to bring healing.[5]

The *Life of Beuno* describes a disciple named Aelhaearn, one of three monk brothers. He was honoured with a chapel at Gwyddelwern near Beuno's church, and has given his name to the settlement of Llanaelhaearn in the Lleyn peninsula, halfway between Beuno's churches of Clynnog and Pistyll. Aelhaearn may have trained in Beuno's monastery at Clynnog. His church and holy well at Llanaelhaearn are beautifully located at the foot of Yr Eifl, a mountain at the neck of the Lleyn peninsula that towers to a height of 564 metres.

Inside the church is a sixth-century memorial stone inscribed in Latin, *Aliortus Elmetiaco hic iacet*, or 'Here lies Aliortus, (a man) from Elmet'. Elmet was a distant

58. A man from Leeds.

Celtic kingdom around Leeds. A family from the Leeds area settling in the Lleyn peninsula must have been even more unusual in Celtic times than it would be today, giving rise to this unique Celtic epitaph. It hints at a group displaced from northern Britain in the face of Saxon conquest. Early written sources preserve a similar tradition. In the churchyard, another Romano-Celtic grave marker commemorates a Christian named Melitus.[6] It is possible that Aelhaearn baptised these two men. The few clues that survive from the time of Beuno and his followers provide us with a fascinating glimpse of their life and work.

CHAPTER ELEVEN

WINIFRED'S HEALING WELLS

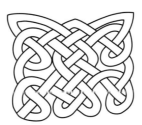

The name Winifred means 'radiant Freda' (or *gwen Frewi* in Welsh). In north Wales, Winifred's cult is ancient and widespread, but surprisingly little is known about her. When Winifred's relics were taken to Shrewsbury abbey in 1138, its monks wrote the *Legend of St Winifred*. She is described as a princess who was beheaded by Caradoc, the son of a neighbouring prince, whom she had refused to marry. A spring flowed at Holywell where her head fell to the ground, but her uncle, Beuno, restored her to life. The legend is one of many in which a saint is decapitated and a healing spring flows where their blood touches the earth. The head, not the heart, was revered as the source of life by Celtic peoples.

Winifred is said to have established a convent of nuns at Holywell. Her spring was known for its healing properties, and attracted pilgrims. Successive English kings honoured Winifred: King Henry V walked from Shrewsbury to Holywell in 1416 to give thanks for his success at the Battle of Agincourt.[1] Lady Margaret Beaufort, mother of Henry VII, rebuilt the Norman chapel over the well, enclosing the spring within a star-shaped pool (see overleaf). With her husband, she rebuilt a number of churches in north Wales, and ordered the construction of another stellate well-chamber at Ffynnon Fair (St Mary's Well) near Cefn, north-west of Denbigh.[2] At Holywell, pilgrims could bathe in a rectangular pool. In the chapel roof, a corbel depicts a medieval pilgrim carrying a sick man on his shoulders, to immerse him in the water. The chapel and well form the best-preserved medieval pilgrimage centre in Britain.

After the Reformation, pilgrims flocked to Holywell, in spite of persecution by the anti-Catholic authorities. Jesuit priests lived here in hiding and secretly celebrated the Eucharist in the town's inns. A Jesuit named John Gerard described his pilgrimage to Holywell in 1593: 'Once I was there on November 3, St Winifred's feast. . . . There was a hard frost at the time, and though the ice in the stream had been broken by people crossing it the previous night, I still found it very difficult to cross with my horse the next morning. But frost or no frost, I went down into the well like a good pilgrim. For a quarter of an hour I lay down in the water and prayed. When I came out, my shirt was dripping, but I kept it on and pulled all my clothes back over it, and was none the worse for my bathe.'[3]

59. Winifred's spring at Holywell.

In the eighteenth century, groups of pilgrims from Lancashire crossed the River Mersey by ferry, then walked up over the Wirral. They waited for low tide and crossed the treacherous sands of the Dee estuary on foot. Eventually they climbed the narrow valley to St Winifred's well. On their return journey, they lit beacons on the Wirral to signal for a boat to ferry them north again. In 1870 the town council opened a hospice for pilgrims; many continue to come for healing.[4]

According to her *Life*, when Beuno left Holywell and headed westwards along the coast, Winifred travelled 7 miles inland with a group of nuns, and settled for a while beside the home of a monk named Deifor at Bodfari. The settlement's name, *Bod Deifor*, means 'Deifor's dwelling'. Marcella, his sister, is commemorated at Whitchurch, 4 miles to the south-west; this became the mother church of Denbigh. The name Whitchurch often indicates an ancient foundation of some importance: it describes a church built of stone at a time when most were constructed of timber. Deifor's church (see p. 90) is on the side of a hill above the Roman road from Chester to Caerhun, which was a fort guarding the River Conwy. There was a Roman station at Bodfari, and a small settlement. The Normans rededicated Deifor's church to St Stephen.

60. Ancient landing stage below Holywell.

A thirteenth-century manuscript mentions Deifor's well, 100 metres down the road from his church, opposite the site of the Roman station. The well can be seen within a concrete surround, beside the road. Even after the Reformation, villagers went in procession from the church down to the well, where the litany, the ten commandments, the epistle and gospel were read. The poorest person in the parish offered a chicken after walking nine times round the well: a cock for a boy or a pullet for a girl. Children were also 'dipped to the neck at three of its corners, to prevent their crying at night'.

Winifred's *Life* relates that after leaving Bodfari, she continued travelling southwest for 7 miles until she reached the church of Sadwrn at Henllan. Sadwrn is Welsh for Saturninus; this saint was educated in the Romano-British Church of south Wales, and was said to be a brother of Illtud. He was known as 'Farchog' (or 'the Knight'). He married a kinswoman, a Breton princess named Canna. They ended their days on Anglesey, where Sadwrn founded a church at Llansadwrn, 3 miles west of Beaumaris. His tombstone, dating from about 530, is set in the chancel wall. It is written in Latin and was carved in Roman capitals by his immediate followers. It reads: 'Here lies blessed Saturninus and his saintly wife. Peace be with you both.'[5]

61. Bodfari church, built into the hillside.

62. Henllan church tower.

Henllan church is set on a hilltop at a crossroads. Its name means 'old, or former, church': it evidently fell into disuse, but was later rebuilt.[6] Perched above a small valley carved out by a stream, the foundations of the early church were apparently too insecure to bear the weight of a stone tower, so in the fourteenth century a tower was built on a rocky outcrop further up the hill; its heavy oak door is still in place. The church was restored in the nineteenth century. The font and a single pillar from the medieval church stand outside the modern porch.

63. Early Christian gravestone, Gwytherin.

At Sadwrn's suggestion, Winifred is said to have travelled 15 miles further into the mountains to the remote settlement of Gwytherin, where a monk named Eleri had founded a small monastery. His mother, Theonia, was its first leader. Gwytherin was already a holy place: above a burial mound, a pair of yew trees now over 2,000 years old were planted on an east–west axis, aligned with the rising and setting sun.[7] Between them is a row of four pre-Christian standing stones. In the fifth or sixth century, one of these was re-used as a tombstone by a Christian family, for inscribed on it in Latin is '(The stone of) Vinnemaglus, son of Senemaglus'.

Near this spot, Eleri founded his community, and in time Winifred succeeded Theonia as its leader. Winifred died here, and in the eighth century her bones were enshrined in a house-shaped wooden reliquary decorated with ornamental metalwork. The story of the Norman monks who took her relics to Shrewsbury abbey has been re-worked by Ellis Peters in the first of her *Cadfael Chronicles*, entitled *A Morbid Taste for Bones*.[8] Gwytherin's little church dates from the nineteenth century, but a late Celtic grave slab inscribed with a cross is set in the chancel step, and nearby is a medieval chest for offerings to Winifred's shrine, carved from a single tree trunk.

There appears to have been a flourishing monastery at Gwytherin in medieval times. It was described as a double community for both monks and nuns, and a survey of 1334 mentions abbots at Gwytherin. The churchyard was larger than it is today; it

64. Winifred's well, Woolston.

included Winifred's *capel y bedd*, or chapel of her grave. The antiquarian Edward Lhuyd wrote that it was still standing in the seventeenth century; it was demolished early in the following century.[9]

Woolston is a small village 4 miles south-east of Oswestry, and it has been suggested that Winifred's well commemorates a stage in the progress of her relics from Gwytherin to Shrewsbury. From Woolston it would have been a day's journey to Shrewsbury. However, the well is likely to be much older. The water flows through stone troughs, to create pools for bathing. The water healed wounds, bruises and broken bones. People with eye diseases visited a spring lower down the water course.[10]

The site may have been a medieval moot, where people gathered to administer justice, for a courthouse is built over the well, dating from the sixteenth or seventeenth century. It is a charming half-timbered building in a secluded copse at the end of a leafy lane. In early times, gatherings to enact laws were held at a significant site such as a mound or a group of standing stones, a holy well or an ancient oak tree.[11] To find the well, coming from Oswestry, turn left into the village and, as the road bends right, walk left down a lane marked 'access to houses only'. At the end of the track, the footpath to the well is through a gate on the right.

Winifred is one of the few female Celtic saints who was widely and consistently venerated through medieval times and into the present day. Her name suggests that, like Brigit (see Chapter Three), Winifred took over attributes of the Celtic goddess of brightness. Although the cult of Brigit was more popular and widespread in Ireland and Scotland, devotion to Winifred remained strong in England and Wales. Even today, her shrine at Holywell is seldom without pilgrims.

CHAPTER TWELVE

CADFAN AND THE BRETON MISSIONARIES

The twelfth-century *Book of Llandaff* describes a Breton monk named Cadfan who sailed to mid-Wales in the sixth century with twelve followers, and settled beside a spring on the sea shore at Tywyn, halfway between Barmouth and Aberystwyth. Here they founded a monastery and were joined by many brothers. A chapel dedicated to Cadfan stood at the north-east end of the churchyard until 1620; it may have contained his shrine. Cadfan's holy well was north-west of the church, and can now be found in the grounds of the NatWest Bank. The spring was visited for healing until long after the Reformation. Baths and changing rooms were built alongside it; they were pulled down in 1894, by which time they had fallen into disuse.[1]

Inside the church, an eighth-century grave-marker commemorates two women from leading families, and may also indicate the burial place of Cadfan, since it reads: 'Beneath a similar mound lies Cadfan; sad that it should enclose the praise of the earth. May he rest without blemish.' This is one of the earliest examples of written Welsh; until this point, inscriptions were normally in Latin. The inscribed panels are set low down on the shaft, perhaps to be read while kneeling. Two successive wooden churches were burnt by Vikings. By the mid-tenth century, St Cadfan's had become the mother church of the area. The present church dates from the late eleventh and early twelfth centuries (shown overleaf).

Cadfan is said to have established a monastery on Bardsey Island, off the tip of the Lleyn peninsula. The Welsh name for Bardsey is Ynys Enlli (Island in the Current). It lies only 2 miles offshore, but because of the strong currents in the Sound, the sea journey can be as much as 6 miles. It is not known whether a monastery was continuously occupied on Bardsey in Celtic times; it may have been used only as a Lenten retreat by monks living on the mainland at Aberdaron, or at nearby Capel Anelog, where two gravestones were found dating from the late fifth or early sixth century. The tombstones refer to two priests and 'many brothers'.[2]

65. Cadfan's church, Tywyn.

66. Bardsey Island from Brach-y-Pwll.

On Bardsey, graves which may be those of early monks are clustered around the ruined tower of a thirteenth-century Augustinian monastery. There are also circular foundations of monks' huts, but these are of indeterminate date. The earliest contemporary reference to the monastery is a record of the death of a monk in 1011. The steward of the thirteenth-century community was given the title *Oeconomus*, an early Greek word originating with the desert monks of the east. This archaic title was probably used by Celtic monks on Bardsey.[3] Several types of herb still grow around the houses on the island, perhaps descendants of those grown by the monks.[4]

Bardsey is a Norse name meaning 'Bardr's Island': in the tenth century it may have become the base of a Viking pirate chief. If so, the monks would have fled, or been killed or kidnapped. They appear to have returned, however, for the lower half of a cross dating from the late tenth or early eleventh century depicts a monk wearing a pleated robe which almost reaches his ankles.[5] In medieval times, Bardsey was called the 'Isle of the Saints' after the monks who were buried here; it became a famous centre for pilgrimage. Today, hermits once more live and pray on the island.

Close to the tip of the Lleyn peninsula, the church at Aberdaron is dedicated to two of Cadfan's followers, Hywyn and Lleuddad. Hywyn was said to have been Cadfan's steward, and chaplain to the monks on the island. Lleuddad is said to have succeeded Cadfan as abbot of Bardsey. A field on the island was known as 'Lleuddad's Garden'; on the mainland, a cave at Aberdaron is named after him, and a well in Bryncroes parish, 4 miles east of Aberdaron. Its water was renowned for curing sick people and animals.[6]

67. Aberdaron church.

As the photograph on the previous page shows, the lower course of the church at Aberdaron has been buried by drifting sand. It has a Norman porch, and by the twelfth century it had a sanctuary seat: this was a stone chair in which those taking refuge from the law could claim immunity, before sailing to safety in another land. This was a *clas* church: a monastery without a rule, whose headship was hereditary. The Normans destroyed the *clas* system because they preferred to control the churches in their territory, but because of its remoteness Aberdaron remained a *clas* church until the Reformation. In the fifteenth century, the church was doubled in size, to accommodate pilgrims.

It is often said that after the Saxon King Ethelfrith massacred twelve hundred monks at Bangor-is-y-Coed on the River Dee, he destroyed their monastery, and the surviving monks fled to Bardsey. However, this statement cannot be traced back beyond the early nineteenth century.[7] Great numbers of pilgrims made the difficult crossing to Bardsey throughout medieval times. Christians travelled along the Lleyn peninsula, stopping at Clynnog Fawr and Pistyll (see Chapter Ten), and at other villages en route. Pilgrims spent the final night before their sea-crossing at Aberdaron.

The hospice where they slept is named 'The Great Kitchen' (*Y Gegin Fawr*); the present building dates from about 1300. Here pilgrims could rest in comfort before their rough journey by sea. There were two embarkation points near Aberdaron: one of

68. The Great Kitchen, Aberdaron.

these was Brach-y-Pwyll (see p. 96), where the foundations of a chapel are visible in the turf above the shore. On the beach is Ffynnon Fair (St Mary's Well), a freshwater spring visible at low tide. Here travellers filled their water bottles before setting sail.

One of Cadfan's followers was said to be St Trillo, who perhaps came ashore at Llandrillo-yn-Rhos (or Church of Trillo on the promontory), now a suburb of Colwyn Bay. Trillo's chapel is situated improbably below the Victorian promenade. Inside the tiny thirteenth-century building, in front of the altar, is a rectangular pool. This encloses the freshwater spring that Trillo or his unknown follower used for drinking, bathing and baptising converts. Beside the chapel are remains of his circular hut.

After living beside the sea, Trillo or his disciples apparently continued inland over the moors, for 30 miles south, near Corwen, is another settlement named Llandrillo.[8] Its church was built beside an ancient yew tree, and on the opposite bank of the river that runs through the village is Trillo's well, at the foot of a large oak. Two stories about the well illustrate how saints were believed to punish those who did not treat their wells with reverence. This spring was originally in the corner of a low-lying field, but in about 1855 the tenant farmer objected to 'trespassers' visiting the well. It therefore ran dry, and reappeared in a neighbouring farmer's field! In another story, the well dried up because someone threw a dead cat or dog into it. By 1913, the spring no longer flowed, except in winter or after heavy rain.[9]

69. Chapel on the shore, Llandrillo-yn-Rhos.

70. The pointed stone in the icy corner.

Five miles north-east of Trillo's inland church is the small town of Corwen, whose name means 'stone church' (or literally, choir-white). This is a Welsh version of the English name Whitchurch which, as we saw in Chapter Eleven, denoted an important stone-built church at a time when others were more simply constructed of timber. Corwen's church is dedicated to two more of Cadfan's followers, Mael and Sulien.

Corwen is at the foot of the Berwyn Mountains, beside the fast-flowing River Dee. It grew beside an important route for travellers through the centuries. Welsh drovers herded their cattle along what later became the A5, the former main road from London to Holyhead. The church at Corwen was built on an ancient holy site, beside a prehistoric standing stone, named in Welsh 'the pointed stone in the icy corner'. When the church was enlarged in medieval times, the ancient stone was incorporated into the wall of the porch.[10]

In the churchyard is a large Bronze Age boulder with seven cup-marks. The boulder was 'Christianised' some time between the ninth and the twelfth century, and used as the base for a tall cross. Another church honours Mael and Sulien in the village of Cwm, 5 miles from the Flintshire coast. Here, the holy well beside their church was visited by those with eye diseases.[11] There are churches dedicated to Sulien in Brittany, and Luxulyan in Cornwall is also named after him.

CHAPTER THIRTEEN

The Dynasty of Dunawd and Deiniol

In Celtic times, families from what is now southern Scotland migrated to north Wales, sometimes for political reasons. Among the immigrants was King Pabo, who fled south with his wife after being defeated in battle by the Picts. King Cyngen of Powys received them kindly, and their friendship was consolidated by a royal marriage: Pabo's daughter, Arddun, married Cyngen's son and successor, Brochwel.

Cyngen gave Pabo land, and the newcomers settled in Anglesey, where they were said to have founded Llanbabo church above Lake Alaw, in the centre of northern Anglesey. The settlement is now deserted: a few ruined cottages surround the small church. Pabo died in the early sixth century. One account relates that, together with his wife, he is buried in the churchyard at Llanerchymedd, a village three miles to the south-east, but according to another tradition the royal tomb was at Llanbabo, where Pabo lies buried with his son and daughter.

The present church (overleaf) dates from the fourteenth century, and at this time a grave slab was carved with an effigy of Pabo portrayed as a medieval monarch. He wears an elegant full-length tunic; a crown and sceptre indicate his royal status. Around the edge of the tombstone, an inscription describes him as 'Pabo Post Pryden', or 'Pabo, Pillar of the northern Britons'. Our word 'British' comes from the Celtic word *Pridani*, which described these northern tribes.

Pabo's son Dunawd became a monk, and founded a large monastery beside the River Dee, 4 miles south-east of Wrexham, at Bangor-is-y-Coed (Bangor under the woods). King Cyngen provided generously for the monastery, as did his son Brochwel, who was Pabo's son-in-law. The monastery is thought to have been somewhere between the present village and the racecourse a mile to the south-west. In 731 Bede wrote of it: 'There were so many monks that they were divided into seven groups, each with its own superior. Each group contained no fewer than three hundred men, who all lived by the work of their own hands.'[1] The flat, fertile plain of the River Dee provided the farmland necessary to support such a large community.

71. King Pabo's church, Llanbabo, Anglesey.

72. The River Dee at Bangor-is-y-Coed.

In about 615 the Saxon King Ethelfrith of Northumbria attacked and defeated the King of Powys, Cyngen's great-grandson, in a battle near Bangor-is-y-Coed. The monks climbed a nearby hill to pray for victory, but many of them were also slaughtered.[2] By the twelfth century, the monastery was a large ruin. In the thirteenth century, a new church was built of red sandstone, with a fine east window in Decorated style. Around the same time, a packhorse bridge was built beside the churchyard. The River Dee is so broad at this point that it was crossed only by boat before that time. The sole reminder of the Celtic monastery is a carved slab 3 metres long, decorated with curving tendrils. It was part of a high cross, and was found in a field a few hundred metres upstream from the church. It can now be seen beside the chancel step.

Abbot Dunawd's three sons helped him to establish his great monastery, and a number of churches in the surrounding countryside are dedicated to Dunawd's son, Deiniol, or Daniel in English. He later left his father's community to establish one of his own. Deiniol travelled west through the mountains, and Maelgwyn, Prince of Gwynedd, gave him land beside the Menai Strait, opposite Anglesey. Deiniol enclosed the site by driving posts into the ground and weaving branches between them. The noun *bangor* means 'the binding part of a wattle fence', and the monastery took its name, Bangor, from its surrounding palisade. Dunawd's foundation had been similarly named, and there was another Bangor beside Belfast Lough in northern Ireland.

Deiniol's community was destroyed by the Vikings in 1073; again, all that remains are geometric carvings from a few stone slabs. Deiniol's church became a cathedral at the centre of one of Britain's earliest dioceses. His son, also called Deiniol, has given his name to a small settlement across the Menai Strait in Anglesey, Llanddaniel Fab (or Church of Daniel the Younger). The village lies just south of the Holyhead Road, and 2 miles from the Menai Strait. Unlike Deiniol's magnificent fourteenth-century cathedral, his son's church (see overleaf) is hidden behind a row of houses in the village that bears his name.

Tysilio was a younger son of Brochwel, King of Powys, and the last prince-monk among Pabo's descendants. The name Tysilio means 'dear Sunday's child', so he was probably born on a Sunday. He lived in the early seventh century, a generation after Deiniol. Tysilio apparently studied under a hermit named Gwyddfarch at the monastery of Meifod in central Wales, 5 miles north-west of Welshpool. This became the mother church of the area, and a burial place for the kings of Powys. Deep beneath the chancel of the church, a vaulted grave was discovered, with a fine carved coffin slab. It can be seen in Meifod church, and probably marked the tomb of a prince of Powys.[3]

The twelfth-century poet Cynddelw described Tysilio building an impressive church at Meifod:

> He raised a church with fostering hand;
> a church with bright lights,
> and a chancel for offerings,
> a church above the stream, by the glassy waters,
> a church of Powys, paradise most fair.[4]

73. Llanddaniel Fab, Anglesey.

74. Llantysilio Mountain.

The boundaries of Powys at this time are not known. The principal royal court was at Shrewsbury, and chieftains travelled between their various courts and halls, since no one place could provide food indefinitely for a lord and his retinue. There was another royal fort near Meifod and, between the two, a fortress at Dinas Bran, towering high above Llangollen and the River Dee. It may be that the royal family of Powys encouraged Tysilio as a monk, for a number of churches dedicated to him are close to royal forts.[5] Llantysilio mountain (see previous page) rises to the north-west of Llangollen. The River Dee flows at its foot, and a church dedicated to Tysilio is built on the valley slope, above the river.

On the opposite side of Llantysilio mountain is another settlement whose church is dedicated to Tysilio. Its name is Bryneglwys, or 'hill church'. The village lies close to the stream in the foreground of the photograph below, and the church is just visible within its hilltop enclosure, on a low shoulder of Llantysilio Mountain. The stream is a tributary of the Dee, which acted as a highway for travel through north Wales and out to sea. The first church at Bryneglwys was replaced by a later Celtic church of stone; some of its boulders can be seen in the west wall of the present church, which was built in about 1570. Many of its wooden furnishings are Jacobean.

There are two more churches named after Tysilio in south Wales, and another

75. Bryneglwys.

to the south-east in the Wye Valley; these were perhaps established by monks from his monastery in Meifod. Tysilio's *Life* was written by a Breton monk in the fifteenth century, but it is unreliable, and may be a conflation of stories about two different men. We are left knowing very little about the activities of the prince-monk of Powys.

At some point in his life, Tysilio is said to have become a hermit on a tiny island named after him, in the Menai Strait. It can be visited by walking down through the woods, a little beyond the Anglesey end of the Menai Bridge. A single-chambered church dating from the fifteenth century probably stands on the site of a Celtic chapel. The islet is reached by a causeway, from which one can watch curlews, oystercatchers and a colony of terns. In Spring, the island is golden with primroses.

Behind the church are the Swellies, dangerous tidal currents. An eighteenth-century traveller, Thomas Pennard, described how 'as a very young man, I ventured myself in a small boat into the midst of the boiling waves and mill-race current.'[6] The next settlement along the coast is Llanfairpwllgwyngyll, whose full name describes both the Swellies and Tysilio's tiny church. When translated it reads: 'Church of St Mary by the pool with the white hazels, near the fierce whirlpool by the church of St Tysilio, near the red cave.' In spite of continuous traffic over the Menai Bridge, Llandysilio Island has retained its peaceful atmosphere through the centuries.

76. Llandysilio Island.

PART III

SCOTLAND

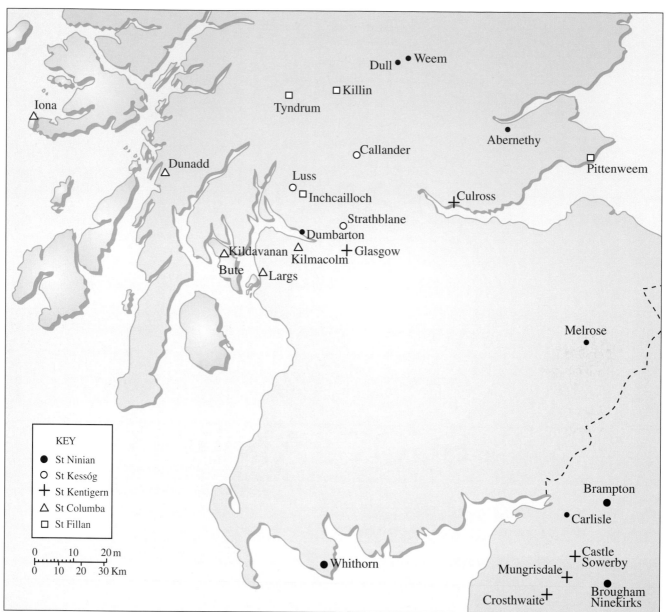

Map 3: Saints of Scotland

KEY
● St Ninian
○ St Kessóg
+ St Kentigern
△ St Columba
□ St Fillan

Iona
Dull ● ● Weem
□ Killin
Tyndrum
Abernethy
Dunadd
Callander
Pittenweem
Luss
□ Inchcailloch
Culross
Strathblane
Dumbarton
△ Kildavanan △ Glasgow
Bute Kilmacolm
△ Largs
Melrose
Brampton
Carlisle
Castle Sowerby
Mungrisdale
Whithorn
Crosthwaite
Brougham Ninekirks

0 10 20 m
0 10 20 30 Km

CHAPTER FOURTEEN

NINIAN, AN EARLY NORTHERN SAINT

We know very little about the fifth-century saint Ninian, except that he worked in Galloway, in south-west Scotland. Writing three hundred years later, Bede tells us that Ninian studied in Rome, before settling at *Candida Casa*, or 'the white house'.[1] Its name suggests that it was built of stone in the Roman style, rather than in the Celtic style. Excavation has provided evidence of successive churches on the site dating from the sixth, seventh and eighth centuries.

Bede tells us that Ninian dedicated his monastery to Martin of Tours. Martin had developed monastic life in Gaul, after learning how monks lived in the Near East. Bede's statement may be supported by the discovery at Whithorn of fragments of early pottery from the Tours region. The pottery found at Whithorn indicates contact with Europe over a long period: fragments from the Mediterranean dated to *c.* 500, Gaulish pieces from *c.* 550 and Frankish and Gaulish plain ceramic ware from *c.* 600.[2] An early fifth-century memorial stone at Whithorn is carved in a style developed in Gaul. It was erected for a man named Latinus by the descendants of Barrovadus, who may have been a local chieftain. It perhaps marks the donation of this site to the Church.

Ninian is said to have used a cave as a quiet retreat (see overleaf). It is on the seashore 5 miles south-west of Whithorn, and is approached by an ancient path. Seven Celtic and Northumbrian crosses are carved on its walls; the earliest of these may pre-date the Northumbrian conquest of Galloway which took place in about 730. This suggests that the cave soon became a place of pilgrimage.

The Anglo-Saxons established a bishopric at Whithorn, constructing a church and a large monastic complex. In the photograph overleaf, wooden posts indicate the outline of the church, built around 750, and beyond it, two timber halls. These would have had bowed walls and curving ridged roofs. The Northumbrians popularised Ninian's cult, to legitimise their control of the Britons in Galloway. One monk wrote a poem about Ninian's life and miracles, and sent a copy to the scholar Alcuin at Charlemagne's court. The Northumbrian thanked him, and sent back a silk veil for Ninian's shrine.[3]

77. Ninian's cave, Whithorn.

78. Site of the Northumbrian church at Whithorn.

Below the chancel of the twelfth-century priory at Whithorn, excavations have revealed the stone coffins of Northumbrian clerics. Fine carved crosses also date from this time, including one whose inscription suggests that it marked a chapel dedicated to St Peter.

In the twelfth century, King David I of Scotland brought the Scottish Church more fully under the control of Rome. He encouraged religious orders to take over native foundations, and Whithorn became a priory of Premonstratensian monks. The Cistercian abbot, Ailred of Rievaulx, who had been educated at King David's court, wrote a *Life of Ninian*,[4] and many new churches were dedicated to Ninian at this time. People continued to visit Ninian's shrine at Whithorn until the sixteenth century. Today, pilgrims once more travel to Whithorn, and walk along the track to Ninian's cave by the seashore.

There are some early churches associated with Ninian in the area around Carlisle in northern Cumbria. Ninian may have been brought up in Carlisle, which was perhaps the centre of a diocese stretching northwards into Galloway. One of the churches associated with Ninian is that of St Martin near Brampton, 9 miles north-east of Carlisle. The tiny church is a mile and a half out of the town, at the end of a road to the right of William Howard School, signed 'Old Church Cemetery'.

79. St Martin's church, Brampton.

The church lies within the site of a Roman camp, one of a series of forts along the Stanegate, constructed before Hadrian's Wall was built. It is situated beside the River Irthing, and was used by a Roman auxiliary unit for a brief period of 25 years; it was abandoned in about AD 150. Amphorae and other artefacts were discovered at the site. The church was probably built soon after the Romans withdrew in the first decade of the fifth century; it hugs the Roman rampart and is not aligned with the camp, but made use of the Roman earthworks for shelter.[5]

It is possible that the church was established by Ninian's followers. There used to be a holy tree here, named St Martin's oak. At the foot of the esker on which the fort was built is a well which may have been a shrine to the local water spirit, since there are signs of a Roman concrete surround. It was later known as 'Ninewells' which may mean Ninian's well' or may derive from the Celtic word *nyen*, or 'holy'. The first graveyard here was oval, following Celtic tradition. The church was rebuilt in Norman times, using some stone from the abandoned fort; only its chancel remains. This is one of the earliest Christian sites in Cumbria.[6]

Brougham Ninekirks, or 'Ninian's church at Brougham' lies 3½ miles east of Penrith, beside the River Eamont. This was the site of the *vicus* or civil settlement which served the Roman fort of Brocavum, 2 miles to the west. The fort guarded a bridge over the River Eamont, where the road from Carlisle to York met the road across the Lake District through Ambleside to Hardknott. Because of its strategic location, the Emperor Hadrian came to Brocavum to inspect his northern defences. Built into the wall of the medieval castle on the site is a fourth-century Christian tombstone recording the death of a soldier aged about thirty-two.[7]

Ninian's church is located in a more peaceful spot, however, where the River Eamont winds through fields. On a clear day, the Pennine peaks are visible, 10 miles further east. The earliest material discovered at the site is eighth-century metalwork, so it is impossible to know whether Ninian's followers worked here. The medieval church on the site is dedicated to the Saxon saint, Wilfred (see Chapter Twenty-four). It was rebuilt in 1660, and contains fine Jacobean woodwork. The oak communion table rests awkwardly on top of the fifteenth-century altar slab, and the socket of a medieval preaching cross stands in the churchyard.

A Manx and Scots Gaelic form of Ninian is Trinian, and there are several churches dedicated to Trinian in northern Scotland.[8] Monks from Whithorn also settled on the Isle of Man, where the ruins of St Trinian's chapel (see overleaf) can be seen beside the road from Douglas to Peel, south-east of Greeba (see map 6). Whithorn was granted land near Greeba in the twelfth century, and the chapel's south door dates from this time. There was an earlier building on the site: a sixth- or seventh-century cross slab survives, while to the right of the altar, paving stones form a plain cross within a circle, and may mark the site of the founder's shrine.

The twelfth-century *Life of Ninian* by Ailred of Rievaulx is too late to be a reliable historical document, but Ailred had access to a lost British *Life of Ninian*, and also travelled to Whithorn to collect stories about him from the Galloway region, which

80. Jacobean pulpit and screen, Brougham Ninekirks.

81. St Trinian's chapel, Isle of Man.

then belonged to Ailred's own diocese of York. Ailred describes how Ninian came into conflict with a ruler named Tudwal, 'King of Man'. He expelled Ninian's followers from his territory, but his crops failed and he became blind. Tudwal repented and sent a servant to Ninian to ask for pardon. Tudwal's sight returned and the drought ended.[9]

Ninian is also said to have worked among the southern Picts, and early dedications in Stirling, continuing north-eastwards to Arbroath, may trace this influence. His monastery at Whithorn became a famous centre of learning and holiness, and remained so for a very long time. A number of leading Irish monks are said to have trained there, and Irish chroniclers used various names to describe it: 'Martin's House' (*Teach Martain*), 'the Little Headland' (*Rosnat*) and 'the Great Monastery' (*Magnum Monasterium*).[10] The community at Whithorn was perhaps the first to forge a significant link between Ireland and Scotland.

CHAPTER FIFTEEN

KESSÓG, A PRINCE FROM CASHEL

Kessóg was a sixth-century prince of Munster in south-west Ireland. He was born in Cashel, in County Tipperary. The rocky outcrop of Cashel was the main stronghold of the kings of Munster from the fourth to the twelfth centuries. St Patrick was said to have visited Cashel in the fifth century, and baptised its reigning king (see Chapter One). Kessóg was one of the numerous Irish monks who left his homeland as an exile for the love of God. He came to south-west Scotland, and evangelised the area around Loch Lomond.

Kessóg founded a monastery on the 'Isle of the Monks' (*Inchtavannach* in Gaelic) in Loch Lomond, a mile south of the town of Luss. Older people still call it 'Isle of the Two Bells' in Gaelic, referring to the bells with which the monks summoned one another to prayer in the chapel. The wooded island is a mile long. In the photograph overleaf, it is viewed from the mainland south of Luss.

Inchtavannach was an ideal location for a monastery: it was sufficiently isolated to afford an opportunity for prayer, but close to the lakeshore, providing easy access to centres of population. Celtic saints selected other islands in Loch Lomond for their homes: further south, Inchmurrin is named after St Mirrin of Paisley, while to the east, Inchcailloch (or Isle of the Old Woman) is dedicated to St Kentigerna, a princess from Leinster, who will be described in Chapter Eighteen.

Kessóg's base on the mainland was at Luss, a settlement which grew beside the mouth of Luss Water, at the point where it flows into Loch Lomond. Kessóg was known as a fine preacher, and he was said to cure the sick with a herb named *lus* in Gaelic. This may refer to the yellow flag which grows near the mouth of Luss Water. The yellow iris appears to have given its name to the settlement. The French word *fleur-de-lys* comes from the same root.[1] Yellow flag is known for its healing properties: infusions made from its leaves were used to staunch bleeding, and the Elizabethan herbalist John Gerard (1545–1611/12) recommended using the strong, spear-shaped leaves as a plaster to cure the effects of bruising.[2] Perhaps Kessóg brought this knowledge with him when he came to settle beside Loch Lomond.

82. Site of Kessóg's island monastery, Loch Lomond.

83. Loch Lomond from Kessóg's church, Luss.

In the churchyard, two sixth-century grave markers, each carved with a Latin cross, and a seventh-century four-holed cross indicate the continued presence of Christians in Luss. An impressive Viking hogback tomb can also be seen in the churchyard, carved with neat rows of imitation roof tiles. It is designed to represent a house of the dead; round its sides, arcading rises from a row of carved columns. The grave slab dates from the Norse invasion led by King Haco of Norway, and is a reminder of one of his most daring raids. In 1263 Haco's longships sailed into the Firth of Clyde and continued northwards through Loch Long. The boats were then hauled overland to Loch Lomond, which lies only 1½ miles to the east. From there the Norsemen proceeded to ravage Luss and much of the surrounding countryside. King Haco then travelled 20 miles round the coast to fight the Battle of Largs. The hogback tomb at Luss commemorates one of his warriors.[3]

Kessóg is said to have worked in the Cumbrae Isles to the west of Largs, and to have travelled eastwards through the Campsie Fells,[4] where he is commemorated at Strathblane, which means 'the strip of land beside the River Blane'. Here a church was erected beside a large standing stone that marks a Bronze Age burial site. The church nestles at the foot of the hills, towards their western end.

Although Strathblane is only 16 miles south-east of Luss, the hills and purple heather create a very different landscape from that around Kessóg's island monastery.

84. Strathblane, in the Campsie Fells.

Lennoxtown is 4 miles to the east of Strathblane, and Kessóg was said to have become bishop of the ancient earldom of Lennox. The present church at Strathblane is modern; far above it towers the rocky outcrop known as 'Earl's Seat'.

North of the Campsie Fells, in Stirling, the Trossachs form a further hilly ridge. The River Teith winds to the south of them, and the town of Callander grew beside a shallow crossing point. A church dedicated to Kessóg once stood here; its walled churchyard can be seen close to the river, beside the road leading into the town. Between the churchyard and a large modern car park is *Tom na Chessaig*, or Kessóg's Mound: a grassy hillock where the monk is said to have gathered the people and preached to them.[5] Beyond the mound, the river broadens as the town narrows below the wooded slopes of the hills.

Kessóg was said to have been murdered by assassins at Bandry, on the shore of Loch Lomond, a mile south of Luss, within sight of the monk's island monastery. Local Christians built a cairn of stones over the place where he fell. This was a pre-Christian custom, and the Celts continued to honour their dead in this way. In his *Life of St Columba*, Abbot Adomnán describes people building a cairn on the spot where a Christian leader has just died.[6]

85. Kessóg's Mound, Callander.

86. Bandry, the site of Kesség's murder.

The cairn at Bandry was destroyed when the shore road was constructed in 1761. A chapel which marked the spot was pulled down in the twentieth century; in its place is a small private car park. A carved stone head, perhaps representing Kessóg, was found when the cairn was destroyed; it now rests on a window ledge in the church at Luss, which continued to be the centre of Kessóg's cult. In 1315, King Robert Bruce declared the church and its surrounding area a place of sanctuary, an offering 'to God and the blessed St Kessóg for ever of three miles round the church as by land and water'.[6] Here criminals could take refuge from the law, and presumably go into hiding on the islands and in the glens.

Kessóg's shrine was visited well after the Reformation. However, one tradition relates that his body did not remain at Luss, but was embalmed in herbs and taken back to Cashel for burial. There are two sixteenth-century references to Kessóg's hand-bell,[7] and the Colquhoun family are hereditary keepers of his *bachuil* or monk's staff. Kessóg is a typical example of a popular local Scottish saint.

CHAPTER SIXTEEN

KENTIGERN, BISHOP OF GLASGOW

Kentigern was a Briton who became Bishop of Glasgow in the sixth century. His name means 'Chief Prince', but we know little about him. We do know that he existed, since his name appears in early texts, but his *Life* was written only in the twelfth century, by a Cumbrian monk named Jocelyn, from Furness abbey. According to legend, Kentigern was the illegitimate son of a British princess. Her angry father set her adrift in a coracle, and she floated across the Firth of Forth, landing on a beach at Culross on the Fife coast. Here, she lit a fire and gave birth to her son.[1]

87. Sunset at Culross.

A sixteenth-century chapel beside the shore at Culross marks the supposed spot where Kentigern was born. It was built by Archbishop Blackadder of Glasgow; only its walls and altar remain. There was an early monastery at Culross, whose abbot, St Serf, was said to have taken the young lad into the community and trained him as a monk. There are traces of an early Celtic church with its altar beneath the imposing ruins of the thirteenth-century Cistercian abbey that crowns the hill above Culross. In a wall adjoining the church tower, a stone cavity housed the reliquary which once contained Serf's bones. The site of the monastery well is in a street below the abbey, and near the shore, sixteenth-century merchants' houses with gabled roofs line the cobbled streets.[2]

It appears that when an anti-Christian chieftain came to power, Kentigern fled southwards, first to Cumbria and then to Wales. His biographer, Jocelyn, describes Kentigern arriving in Carlisle and proceeding to Crosthwaite: 'When he came to Carlisle, he heard how many people in the mountain district were idolatrous and

88. Crosthwaite church porch.

ignorant of God's law. So he turned aside, and converted many from strange beliefs to Christianity, and corrected the errors of believers. He stayed for a while in a wooded area, to encourage and confirm in their faith the people who lived there. He planted a cross there as a symbol of faith, and so it is called Crosthwaite in English.'[3]

Crosthwaite church is on the northern outskirts of Keswick; it looks towards Skiddaw's peak, 2 miles distant. 'Thwaite' is Norse for a forest clearing; it well describes the 'wooded area' mentioned by Jocelyn. The British princes of Strathclyde reoccupied Cumbria from 900 to 1092, and held their territory against both the English and the Norse. They revived an interest in their Glasgow saint, Kentigern, and built churches in the places where he was said to have preached. The earliest remains in Crosthwaite church are from the twelfth century. The church has a unique set of twelve crosses around its inside walls, with another twelve carved on its external walls. These were carved when the church was re-dedicated in 1523, according to the English rite of consecration.

It would have been logical for Kentigern to arrive first at Carlisle, to enquire about the region, for Carlisle was its ancient capital. It was a large town inside the Roman frontier, at the western end of Hadrian's Wall, in a key position on the route north

into Scotland. It is likely that there were Christians in Carlisle from the fourth century onwards, and there was a bishop there from Roman times onwards. One can imagine Kentigern meeting with him before proceeding southwards.

The route to Crosthwaite would have taken Kentigern through Caldbeck and Mungrisdale, both of which have churches dedicated to him. Of the eight medieval churches named after Kentigern in Cumbria, the one at Mungrisdale uses his pet name, Mungo (or My Dear One). The hamlet is situated to the east of Skiddaw's peak, between Keswick and Penrith. The name Mungrisdale may mean 'Valley of Mungo's pigs'; these were a staple food in Celtic times. The tiny church was rebuilt in 1756, and the porch retains its floor of cobblestones.[4]

89. Mungrisdale church porch.

90. Castle Sowerby church.

Castle Sowerby is another ancient site dedicated to Kentigern. There is no village here; only a country house. The church was built at a place where Kentigern was said to have baptised converts; the well, now dry, is in the churchyard wall, beside the track which leads to the church and the house. The church is in a beautiful, though isolated, location, surrounded by farmland and bleak moors. There was originally a small twelfth-century church here, which was enlarged in the sixteenth century and repaired in the eighteenth. Its whitewashed walls gleam in the sunlight.

Castle Sowerby is not on most maps. To find it, leave the M6 at junction 41. Take the B5305 as if for Sebergham. After 6 miles, turn left for Lamonby. Castle Sowerby is then signed. Other Cumbrian churches dedicated to Kentigern can be found at Kirkcambeck and Irthington (north of Carlisle), at Grinsdale, where the River Eden flows into the Solway Firth, and at Bromfield and Aspatria, near the Cumbrian coast. If Kentigern sailed to north Wales, this would have been an easy route.

Jocelyn recounts how Kentigern arrived in Wales and eventually gained permission from Maelgwyn Gwynedd, the ruling prince, to build a monastery at the junction of the Elwy and Clwyd rivers, at a site now named St Asaph in English, and Llanelwy in Welsh. Jocelyn tells how Kentigern 'went through the area, exploring different places,

91. St Asaph Cathedral, Denbighshire.

bearing in mind the air quality, the fertility of the soil, the suitability of the fields, pasture and woodland, and the other requirements for a monastic site.'[5]

Eventually, a wild white boar indicated where Kentigern should build his church. This is a common feature in stories of Celtic saints' foundations, such as those of Ciarán of Saighir (see Chapter Seven) and Cadoc (see Chapter Nine). In each of these accounts, the appearance of a wild boar represents God's choice of the site. Once the location was chosen, 'some cleared the ground and levelled it, while others dug the foundations. They chopped down trees, transported them and hammered planks together to build a church following Kentigern's plan, and made wooden polished furniture, for the British did not yet build in stone.'[6]

We do not know how much Jocelyn reconstructed the story from his own experience of monastic life, but it is possible that Kentigern founded a monastery here. His ablest student was said to be Asaph, a grandson of King Pabo, whom we met in Chapter Thirteen. When the political scene shifted in northern Britain, and Kentigern was able to return to Glasgow, he is said to have left Asaph in charge of his Welsh monastery, and returned north with a large group of monks.[7]

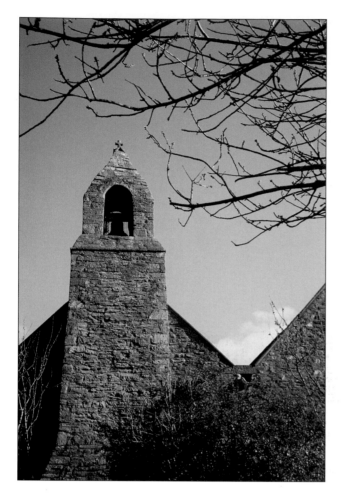

92. Bell turret, Llanasa.

Between St Asaph and the Flintshire coast, the village of Llanasa lies in a sheltered hollow. Its church is dedicated to Asaph and Cyndeyrn (or Kentigern in Welsh). It is possible that this is an early foundation by monks from St Asaph. The present double-chambered church was built in the fifteenth century; an asymmetrical bell turret was constructed at this time. In 1540 when the monasteries were dissolved, two fine stained glass windows were brought to Llanasa church from nearby Basingwerk abbey. The window over the altar depicts four saints, including Beuno dressed as a bishop and his niece, Winifred, with a scar round her throat (see Chapters Ten and Eleven), although Winifred is named, probably wrongly, as St Catherine.[8]

Kentigern is said to have left Wales and returned north at the invitation of Rhydderch Hael (or Roderick the Generous), who regained control of Strathclyde after a savage battle between British chieftains north of Carlisle in 573. Rhydderch established a base on Dumbarton Rock, and Kentigern returned to Glasgow, a little further up the River Clyde. Kentigern is said to have died in his monastery, which stood on the site of Glasgow cathedral.[9] Its well is built into the wall of the cathedral crypt. Nearby, arcading survives from the thirteenth-century shrine that contained Kentigern's relics.

CHAPTER SEVENTEEN

COLUMBA, ABBOT OF IONA

We probably know more about Columba (521–97) than about any other Celtic saint. He was an outstanding man: a scholar, priest and poet, a warrior, prince and politician. Born in Donegal, into the royal family of the northern Uí Néill, he played a significant role in both Irish and Scottish history. Columba studied under a Christian bard in his mother's county of Leinster. He became a monk at an early age, and was given the Latin name Columba, meaning 'dove'. He trained in the monastery of Finnian of Moville, was ordained a priest, and founded his first monastery at Derry in his family's territory in 556. He later established a community at Durrow in central Ireland, and made a number of other foundations. While visiting his former abbot, Finnian of Moville, Columba is said to have borrowed a copy of St Jerome's new Vulgate translation of the Bible, in order to copy out the psalms. He was discovered when he had almost finished, and the abbot demanded the copy. This first recorded breach of copyright was brought before the High King, who ruled in favour of Abbot Finnian.

In 561 the High King invaded Connaght, because a royal hostage who was under Columba's protection had been slain. Fog hampered his attack, and the High King was ambushed and defeated. Clergy fought in battle at this time, and it is likely that as prince and abbot, Columba fought alongside the rest of his clan. He later sailed to Scotland as a 'pilgrim for Christ', but unlike other monks, who travelled with no fixed destination in mind, Columba was probably invited by his relative, Conall, King of Argyll, to help him repel the Picts. Under their ruler, King Brude, the Picts had attacked Argyll, killed Conall's father and driven the Irish settlers westwards to the sea.

Conall's father had built a fortress on a rocky outcrop at Dunadd, 23 miles south of Oban. It rises from flat, boggy land beside the River Add (hence its name: *dún* or fortress by the Add). From the hill-fort, Conall's warriors could attack the Picts, while his warships could command the sea route to Ireland. The fortress is in a central location on the Crinan isthmus, a key point of entry into western Scotland. Dunadd's main entrance is a natural gully through walls of rock; it was closed by great gates with a timber superstructure. A small peak formed an inner citadel. At the age of forty-two, Columba set sail from Ireland with twelve companions. It is possible that he came to

Dunadd to meet King Conall and discuss the dangerous political situation.[1] At some point there was a monastic presence at Dunadd, for a lump of orpiment, a yellow pigment used by monks to illuminate manuscripts, was found there.

93. Entrance to Dunadd fortress.

One tradition relates that Columba was given the island of Iona by King Conall, as a site for a monastery. Iona is 3 miles long, and lies west of the larger island of Mull. We know a considerable amount about life in Columba's community, because in about 690 the ninth abbot of Iona, Adomnán, wrote a *Life of Columba* and preserved for us many details of daily life on the island. The earliest surviving text of the *Life* was written on Iona by Dorbbéne, a monk who succeeded Adomnán as abbot and died in 713. We are fortunate to possess such an early copy, written on goatskin parchment in a heavy Irish hand. Columba lived in a hut built on planks on a small rocky mound in the monastery compound. The mound can still be seen in front of the large Benedictine abbey that was later built on the site. This may also be the 'little hill overlooking the monastery' from which, according to Adomnán, Columba gave his final blessing to the monks before his death.[2]

Adomnán describes the monks walking across the island with their farm implements on their backs, to reach the sandy plain where they grew crops. He tells us of the white horse that carried the milk churns from the cow pasture, and he mentions expeditions to larger islands to fetch wood for building, since there were no trees on Iona. Adomnán pictures the monks writing manuscripts, and praying in the small church, where Columba's clear voice could be heard above the others. He could also be recognised by his white cowl, or hooded cloak, for the other monks wore unbleached cowls.[3]

The *Life* refers to fifty-five sea voyages back and forth between Iona and Ireland. Monks and pilgrims came to visit or to join the community. Those travelling from Scotland crossed the island of Mull and then shouted across the Sound to Iona, for a brother to ferry them over. From his hut on planks, Columba could see them coming. On arrival, guests had their hands and feet washed.

Today there are few remains of Iona's Celtic monastery; St Odhráin's chapel (right) is the earliest building to survive on the island. It dates from the twelfth century, and stands within what was probably the first Christian burial ground on Iona. It is named after an early monk who may have lived here before Columba's arrival. Odhráin's oratory resembles Irish chapels of the period, with a single doorway in the west wall, decorated with chevron and beak-head ornament. It was probably rebuilt as a family burial vault by Somerled, King of the Isles, who died in 1164.[4]

94. Odhráin's chapel, Iona.

In 1979, excavations were carried out in the early seventh-century boundary ditch between the little hill on which Columba's cell was built and Odhráin's cemetery. Objects were discovered that would have been in use at the end of Columba's lifetime, including heeled shoes and other leather goods, and elegant wooden bowls that had been turned on a lathe in the monastic workshops. Clay moulds indicated that fine quality metalwork was produced. There had also been a glass furnace in which glass beads were created, and ornaments of various colours with twisted patterns.[5]

The great rectangular ramparts which surrounded the monastery on Iona can still be traced: they were constructed around the time of Columba's death, and were partly bounded by a hedge of hawthorn and holly. The tiny chapel in front of the Benedictine abbey is also built on Celtic foundations, and may mark the site of Columba's shrine. There are three elaborate high crosses, and a winding path of large stones, known as the 'Street of the Dead'. Chieftains were brought to Iona from the Scottish mainland for burial, and this was the track along which they were solemnly carried.

Outside the great rampart, 300 metres to the north-east, are the remains of another Celtic cemetery, named *Cladh an Disirt* in Gaelic. It was entered through an impressive gateway framed by two large stone pillars (see overleaf). These supported a giant lintel, which has now fallen. The cemetery was enclosed by a wall, and beside it was a hermitage, whose superior is named in a twelfth-century list of monastic officials. There are the remains of a medieval stone chapel beside the entrance to the cemetery.[6]

Columba left Iona from time to time. He returned to Ireland in 575 as adviser to King Conall's successor, to attend an assembly of the northern Irish Uí Néill, which was held in Derry. At this meeting, Columba probably helped to negotiate a new status of independence for the Irish in western Scotland; he also spoke in defence of the Irish bards.[7] He returned to Ireland in 585 to visit his monastery at Durrow, and

95. Celtic hermitage, Iona.

Ciarán's at Clonmacnoise. His enthusiastic welcome there by Abbot Alither was described in Chapter Four.

Columba twice travelled north to Inverness, probably on political missions to confer with Brude, King of the Picts. His first visit was apparently to negotiate peace between King Conall and the Picts, and to ask permission to settle on Iona, which King Brude considered to be in Pictish territory. Columba and his companions sailed up the Great Glen to Inverness, and Adomnán recounts that on the journey they encountered a creature in the River Ness that people have equated with the Loch Ness monster: 'Now the beast . . . was lying hidden at the bottom of the river, but noticing that the water above was disturbed by (the monk) who was crossing, it suddenly emerged and, swimming to the man . . . rushed up with a great roar and open mouth.' Columba ordered the monster to return to the depths, and the monk reached the safety of the boat.[8]

Columba is also said to have travelled southwards to the area around the Firth of Clyde. The normal route from Iona to Strathclyde was by sea, with two short land-crossings: through Crinan Water and past Dunadd, down Loch Fynne and across the Isle of Bute. Columba may have landed on the Scottish mainland at Largs, 11 miles south of Greenock, on the beach below the modern church of St Columba (right). Remains of the medieval Old Kirk can be seen nearby.[9]

It is said that Columba met Kentigern, either in Glasgow or at Kilmacolm, 12 miles to the west. Since Columba's monks preached in Strathclyde, it would have been natural for Columba to seek permission for this from the local bishop. A tradition relates that the two men met beside the Gillburn, that flows past the lower end of

96. The harbour at Largs.

Kilmacolm churchyard. The name of the settlement means 'Cell of my Columba' (or *Cil ma Colum*). The chancel of the thirteenth-century church is incorporated into a much larger modern one (see overleaf).

Columba died on Iona. Adomnán describes the abbot's final tour of the island, when he was pulled in a cart, since he could no longer walk far. He blessed the island, the monks, the barns and the white horse. He returned to his hut and tried to complete a psalm that he was copying, but was unable to do so. That night was Whitsun Eve. Columba went to church for the midnight office, but collapsed there and died. Adomnán described his last hours: 'At midnight, at the sound of the ringing of the bell, (Columba) quickly rises and goes to the church. He runs faster than the others, enters alone, and falls on his knees in prayer beside the altar. Diormit, his attendant . . . entering the church, keeps asking sadly, "Where are you, Father?" And feeling his way in the dark, since the brothers have not yet brought in the lights, he finds the saint prostrate before the altar. He lifts him up a little, sits beside him and rests (Columba's) head in his lap.'

Adomnán continues: 'Meanwhile, the whole community of monks run up with lights, and seeing their father dying, begin to weep. And as we have learnt from people who were there, the saint, whose soul had not yet departed, opens his eyes and

97. Kilmacolm church.

looks around on both sides with wonderful cheerfulness. . . . Then Diormit lifts up the right hand of the saint, in order to bless the monks in choir. . . . And after thus giving his holy blessing, he at once breathed forth his spirit. Meanwhile the whole church was filled with sorrowful weeping.' His monks prayed around him for three days before burying him. They were left to grieve in peace, since storms prevented visitors from crossing the Sound.[10]

From Columba's time onwards, Iona became the centre of Celtic learning. Monks from Ireland and Europe came to study here, and monks from Iona preached among the Picts of eastern Scotland and the Anglo-Saxons of Northumbria. Adomnán was one of the great abbots of Iona. Like Columba, he was a member of the northern Uí Néill. He trained as a monk under Columba's nephew, and became abbot of Iona in 679, at the age of fifty-five. He wrote a book on the Holy Land that was to become a standard guide for pilgrims, although today he is better known for his *Life of Columba*.

Adomnán travelled twice to Northumbria, and spent at least a year in the monastery at Jarrow, where Bede was then a young monk. Bede wrote of the Irishman: 'He was a good and wise man, with a very sound knowledge of the scriptures.'[11] Bede adds that on his return to Iona, Adomnán tried to introduce the Roman method of calculating Easter, but failed to do so. As abbot of Iona and its daughter houses, Adomnán travelled widely in Scotland and Ireland, where in 697 he took part in the Synod of Birr. A product of this gathering was 'Adomnán's Law' (or *Cáin Adomnáin*), which protected women by exempting them from warfare. Boys and clergy were similarly protected, and provision was made for effective sanctuary. Adomnán's Law was upheld in both Ireland and Scotland. The abbot was now seventy; he returned to Iona in 704 and died shortly afterwards.

Adomnán's journeys south-east from Iona to the Scottish mainland and on to Northumbria would have taken him across the Isle of Bute. The island is 15 miles long and only 2½ miles wide at its narrowest point. Boats could therefore be hauled from one side to the other, while the crew could stock up with food and fresh water.[12] Close to this route is Kildavanan (or Cell of Adomnán), a headland where there used to be a chapel dedicated to Adomnán. It is likely to have been the place where he and others used to land, en route from Iona to Lindisfarne. These two communities became focal points for Columba's monastic family: they preserved its traditions, its art and its learning.

Iona suffered a number of Norse raids. In 806, during their third attack, Vikings killed sixty-eight monks, and the remainder of the community decided to transfer to Ireland. They acquired the monastery of Kells in eastern Ireland and from then on, the abbot of Kells was called 'the successor of Columba'. The monks brought their treasures with them including, perhaps, the *Book of Kells*, a magnificently decorated

98. Kildavanan Point, Bute.

gospel book, which was created on Iona in about 800. Its text is a poor version of the Latin gospels; it is interesting that its scholarship does not match the skill lavished on its illustrations. These were executed in the latest Northumbrian style by monks trained at Lindisfarne.

The name Kells derives from the monks' cells at the centre of the settlement. Outside the cathedral, four high crosses survive from the Celtic monastery. The south cross was probably erected soon after the monks came from Iona. It is inscribed 'the Cross of Patrick and Columba'. It stands beside a tenth-century round tower, into which the monks could climb for safety. The tower is 28 metres high, and must have been frequently used, for the monastery was plundered at least seven times before 1006. Most round towers have four windows at the top, so that the monks could keep watch in all directions. Unusually, that of Kells has five windows, each facing one of the five ancient roads that lead to Kells.

To the north-west of the cathedral is Columba's House, which was possibly built by monks from Iona in the ninth century. It is a small church with a basement, through which one enters the building, and walls over 1.2 metres thick. The church has a steeply pitched roof, and between the barrel vault and the roof is an attic or croft divided into three rooms, where monks could work and sleep. One can climb up a steep ladder into the croft: it is not difficult to imagine the monks sleeping comfortably above their little church. This is one of the few buildings that has survived intact from early times.

99. Columba's House, Kells: view into the attic.

CHAPTER EIGHTEEN

FiLLAN, A LEiNSTER PRiNCE

The story of Fillan begins with that of his mother, Kentigerna, and her brother Comgan. Comgan was an eighth-century Irish chieftain, the son of Cellach (or Kelly), Prince of Leinster. Comgan succeeded his father, but was wounded in battle and driven out of his kingdom by a coalition of neighbouring tribes. He fled to Scotland with his family, including his widowed sister, Kentigerna, and her children, one of whom was Fillan. Comgan founded a small monastery at Lochalsh, which is the crossing point for the huge island of Skye. After his death, Fillan buried him on Iona, and built a church in his honour.[1]

Fillan's mother, Princess Kentigerna, had been married to Federach, King of Munster. On her arrival in western Scotland, she preached alongside her brother around Loch Alsh. On the south side of nearby Loch Duich, Kilchintorn (or 'Cell of Kentigerna') is dedicated to her. She ended her days as a hermit, 70 miles south of her brother, on an island near Balmaha on the eastern shore of Loch Lomond (see overleaf). The island is named after her: in Gaelic it is called Inchcailloch, or 'Isle of the Old Woman'. Kentigerna died here in old age in the early eighth century. The ruins of her chapel can be seen on the island.[2] Inchcailloch can be viewed by climbing the steps up the hill in the forest park on the mainland in Balmaha; in summer, boats sail to the island.

Fillan may have trained as a monk in Wexford, before leaving Ireland with his mother's family. After preaching on the Scottish west coast, Fillan travelled eastwards and settled on the coast of Fife. We hear of him living in a cave at Pittenweem. The town's name means 'Place of the Cave': 'Weem' is a transliteration of *uaimh*, which is the Gaelic word for 'cave'. Around the south coast of Fife there are a number of caves where hermits lived: at Dysart, at East Weymss and at Caiplie, a mile east of Pittenweem. A cave was warm in winter and cool in summer, and if it looked out to sea, it encouraged prayer.[3]

Fillan's cave (see overleaf) is a large one, with two outer chambers, the second of which branches into two more. An altar has been erected in the chamber to the right, while in the left-hand chamber there is a freshwater pool: this provided Fillan with drinking water. The rock plug containing the cave stands among fishermen's cottages

100. Dawn over Inchcailloch, Loch Lomond.

101. Fillan's cave, Pittenweem.

102. Dochart Falls, Killin.

on the steep road down to the old harbour. Fillan left his cave to become abbot of a nearby monastery, where he remained for some years.

According to his legend, recorded in the *Aberdeen Breviary*, Fillan felt called to 'wander for God', so he resigned from his monastery and travelled 50 miles eastwards into the Highlands. He settled at the head of Loch Tay in Perthshire, beside the Dochart Falls at Killin (see previous page). He is said to have built a mill here. Monks who trained in Ireland knew how to construct mills and grind flour; they developed a horizontal mill- wheel, and brought their technology with them.

Fillan was said to sit on a stone under an ash tree near the mill at Killin, to preach to the local people. The mill became the focal point of the settlement. In a small community, the miller supervised the sowing of seed and the cutting of peat to fuel the mill's oven, which might also be the village bakery. Fillan's feast day, 9 January, is still a holiday for the mill-workers at Killin.

The ruins of Fillan's church and cemetery at Killin can be seen in the grounds of a large hotel beside the main road. Next door, the modern church houses an eighth-century font, carved from a huge boulder. The seven-sided font may date from the time when Fillan was baptising around the head of Loch Tay.[4]

Left: 103. Celtic font, Killin.

Opposite: 104. Fillan's Pool, Auchtertyre.

Fillan also had a reputation for healing. His eight healing stones have always been kept at Fillan's Mill, which now houses the Breadalbane Folklore Centre. These large black and grey stones, smoothed by the river, were considered to cure different parts of the body. A large skull-shaped stone with two 'eye sockets', for example, was invoked for diseases of the head. People still come to hold Fillan's stones and pray for healing.

Ten miles west of Killin, Fillan is commemorated along Strathfillan, where he died and was buried. East of Tyndrum, where the A82 passes Auchtertyre Farm, a shallow stretch of the River Dochart is named Fillan's Pool (see previous page). It was believed to cure insanity: deranged people were bathed in the river, wrapped in straw, then taken to St Fillan's priory, half a mile to the east. Here they spent the night with their head in the stone font, with Fillan's bell placed above them. Cures were sought into the nineteenth century.[5] The well-trodden grass track leading to the river indicates that the pool is still visited.

Fillan's ruined priory with its walled cemetery can be seen on Kirkton Farm. The monk's bronze hand-bell and his staff, encased in a delicate medieval reliquary, are now in the National Museum of Scotland, Edinburgh. After his death, a bone from Fillan's arm was preserved, and King Robert Bruce asked if he might borrow it from the Abbot of Inchaffray, to have it carried before him into the Battle of Bannockburn, to invoke Fillan's blessing on the enterprise. The cautious abbot agreed, but removed the bone from its reliquary before handing over the empty container. In spite of this, Robert Bruce won the battle!

PART IV

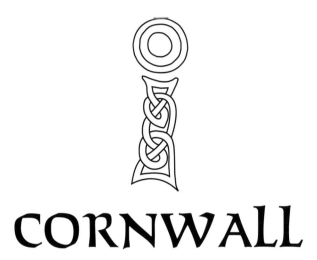

CORNWALL

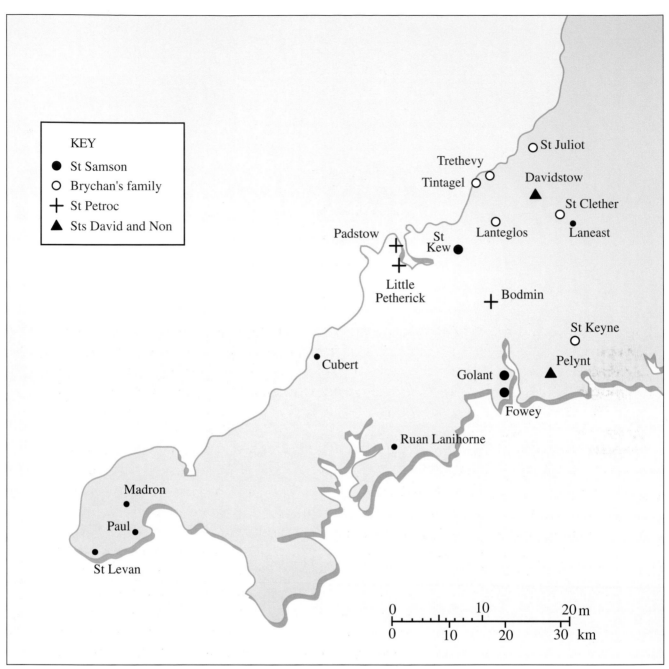

KEY
● St Samson
○ Brychan's family
+ St Petroc
▲ Sts David and Non

St Juliot
Trethevy
Tintagel
Davidstow
St Clether
Laneast
Padstow
St Kew
Lanteglos
Little Petherick
Bodmin
St Keyne
Pelynt
Cubert
Golant
Fowey
Ruan Lanihorne
Madron
Paul
St Levan

0   10   20 m
0   10   20   30   km

Map 4: Saints of Cornwall

CHAPTER NINETEEN

THE TRAVELS OF SAMSON

Samson (*c.* 490–*c.* 565) was a Welsh monk about whom we know a considerable amount, because a long and interesting *Life of Samson* survives. It was written by a Breton monk, perhaps as early as the seventh century. Samson was born of a wealthy family in south-west Wales. His parents took him to St Illtud's famous school at Llanilltud Fawr in the Vale of Glamorgan (see Chapter Nine), where Samson later became a monk. Illtud had been ordained by Bishop Germanus of Auxerre in about 445; he combined Christian, classical and druidic learning, and was trained in scripture and philosophy, poetry and rhetoric, grammar and arithmetic. After this broad education, Samson was ordained a priest, and went to the monastery's daughter house on Caldey Island off the Pembrokeshire coast; in time he became its abbot.

Samson later visited Ireland, where he acquired a chariot, or light cart, in which to travel. He put his cart on a boat and returned to Llanilltud Fawr, where he was invited to become abbot. He was consecrated a bishop in about 521. Nine hundred years later, a wood carver depicted Samson as a bishop. The panel overleaf may once have formed part of a rood screen; it was later used as a section of the fine wooden pulpit in Golant church, near Fowey in Cornwall. Samson carries a gospel book and a bishop's pastoral cross. He is a solid figure, whose furrowed brow reflects the cares of his office. He stands with dignity, his head framed in a recess which also forms a halo.

Samson decided to leave his native Wales and travel as a pilgrim for Christ, so he sailed to Cornwall, together with his relatives and servants. They landed at Padstow and continued up the Camel estuary until they came within 2 miles of the monastery of Landocco, now named St Kew. This was probably a daughter house of Llandough in south Glamorgan; it is the earliest recorded Cornish monastery. A tall Celtic cross in St Kew churchyard dates from the time of the monks, and a holy well in the wall of the former vicarage (see overleaf) was probably the monks' water supply. It was much visited by pilgrims; its well-house was restored in 1890.[1]

The author of Samson's *Life* describes how the bishop had hoped to stay at Landocco, but the community sent one of their number, Juvanius, to dissuade him. The monks had become lax, he explained, and did not wish to be condemned by the

105. Carving of Samson on Golant pulpit.

106. St Kew holy well.

107. Gravestone, St Kew monastery.

bishop. Juvanius also implied that the community would not take kindly to criticism from an outsider. Juvanius politely presented his case: 'Most loving father, the journey you have undertaken is desirable for a servant of God, who in the gospel praises those who become pilgrims for his sake. But your request to stay with us is not convenient. Otherwise, we who are unworthy, might condemn you. Or, more to the point, you might condemn us as we deserve. For I wish you to know this, that we have lapsed from our former rule.'[2]

The community at St Kew may have fallen from their former ideals, but they were well educated. The monks could read both Irish Gaelic and Latin, as we know from a bilingual grave marker which has survived from the early monastery. This is a rounded pillow stone, which marked the head of a grave. The mason carved the name of the dead man in Latin, writing 'IUSTI', which means '(the stone of) Justus', and enclosed the name within a roughly carved cartouche. Along the edge of the gravestone, the mason inscribed the man's name in Irish ogham, a stroke alphabet which was used frequently in south-east Ireland, but rarely in Cornwall. The pillow stone can be seen inside the church.

Samson and his party continued southwards across Cornwall. As they travelled, they met a group of pagan people with their chieftain, celebrating the mysteries of their ancestors. A large standing stone dominated the scene. Samson challenged them, with little success, until a boy galloped past in a horse race which was perhaps a feature of the assembly, and was thrown from his mount. He seemed dead, but Samson prayed beside him for two hours, and the lad recovered. Samson carved a cross on the standing stone, and the author of his *Life* adds: 'I myself have been on that mountain, and with my own hand have reverently touched the sign of the cross which St Samson carved by hand with an iron tool on the stone that stands there'.[3] Crosses incised like this on ancient sacred stones were the forerunners of the elaborate Celtic crosses executed in the following centuries.

After Samson cured the boy who had been thrown from his horse, the ruler told his followers to come and have their baptism confirmed by Samson. This implies that they were already Christian. The chieftain then asked Samson if he could solve another of their problems: an evil serpent inhabited an impenetrable cave, and terrorised the neighbourhood. Samson agreed to visit the 'terrible cave', and the cured boy showed him the way. Samson drove the serpent out of the cave and killed it. The grateful chief and his followers asked Samson to become their bishop. He refused, but accepted the offer of the cave as a retreat.[4]

Samson's cave can be seen at Golant, down by the harbour. It is beside the railway track, and although the entrance is covered by brambles in the summer, it can easily be located behind the third telegraph pole alongside the track. It is a long cavern, and can be explored only with wellingtons and a torch, but Samson's biographer even has an explanation for the water that floods the cavern: 'One day (Samson) was thirsty. . . . After he had prayed, he saw water dripping in a continuous shower from the rocky roof of the cave . . . and to this day that water does not cease flowing, day or night.'[5]

108. Samson's cave, Golant.

109. Samson's well, Golant church.

Golant may derive its name from the Cornish for 'festival valley'. Professor Charles Thomas suggests that an annual festival was perhaps held to celebrate the settlement's deliverance from the serpent's power.[6] Golant church is high above the harbour and the cave. It contains the fine pulpit illustrated earlier, and a representation in modern stained glass of events from Samson's life, including his encounter with the 'poisonous and most evil serpent'. Close to the church porch is Samson's holy well in a medieval roofed well-house.

Half a mile to the west is Castle Dore hill-fort, where the chieftain and his followers may have lived. It was defended by two well-preserved circular ramparts; inside, there were many round houses. The fortress can best be approached from the B3269, by walking along the track to Lawhibbet Farm. The fort is in the first field to the right. Paul Aurelian, another early monk whom we will meet in Chapter Twenty-two, is described as visiting a ruler named Mark and styled Cunomorus (or Sea Dog), probably at Castle Dore. Cunomorus is named on a sixth-century pillar stone found nearby: it can be seen beside the road as it leads into Fowey. The son of Cunomorus was named Drustan: the two men may have become King Mark and his nephew Sir Tristan in the later legend of King Arthur.

110. Norman font, Fowey.

Samson continued 2 miles southwards to Fowey. Here he probably established a monastery on land given to him by the chieftain who had been so impressed by his powers. Fowey's large natural harbour made it an ideal departure point for Brittany, and the church is near the shore. The present building dates from the fourteenth and fifteenth centuries, but the font from the earlier Norman church survives. It is carved out of hard black elvan stone from a quarry near Padstow. It was transported along the same route that Samson followed. One section of the font was left undecorated; perhaps the mason died before completing his task.

Samson left his father Amon in charge of the community at Fowey, and sailed to Brittany with his followers. He established Dol on the north coast and several other monasteries. He signed the decrees of Church Councils in Paris in 553 and 557. On one of his journeys to Paris, a wheel fell off his much-used chariot. Samson took an active part in Breton politics, and has dedications in eastern Brittany and Normandy. A town in Guernsey and one of the Scilly Isles is named after him.

CHAPTER TWENTY

THE FAMILY OF BRYCHAN

In Celtic times, Irish families emigrated to south Wales in search of land. In the fifth century, the family of Brychan landed in south-west Wales and travelled east along ancient routeways to the hilly region of Brecon, where they settled. The name Brecon is derived from Brychan. We hear about his life in a document possibly dating from early times that tells how his mother, Marcella, returned to Ireland during a severe winter in order to marry an Irish prince. The frost killed many of the warriors who accompanied Marcella, but her father had a fur cloak made for her, and she arrived safely. She gave birth to a son before returning home and named him Brychan, which means 'little badger'.[1]

In time, Brychan became the ruler of Brecon. He was said to have married three times, and had many children. Ancient lists record twelve sons and twelve daughters, although different versions include different names. Churches dedicated to Brychan's children are found in Wales, south-east Ireland, Cornwall and Brittany. Some of these may date from early times, but Brychan was popular in the Middle Ages, and many more churches were then named after his family. Traditions about Brychan in south-west England are enshrined in a *Life of Nectan*, written in the twelfth century at Hartland abbey, close to Barnstaple Bay in north Devon.[2]

The story portrays Nectan as the eldest of Brychan's children, although Welsh accounts do not include Nectan's name. The abbey claimed to have discovered Nectan's relics, and his shrine became well known. At Trethevy near Tintagel, on the north Cornish coast, Nectan's Kieve is a waterfall tumbling into a wooded glen, where the River Trevillitt flows towards the sea. 'Kieve' is Cornish for 'bowl', and describes the pool enclosed by rocks beneath the waterfall. At the top of the falls are the lower courses of what may have been a medieval chapel dedicated to Nectan (see overleaf). Its walls are a metre thick; the timbered superstructure was added in 1860. The local story is that Nectan lived as a hermit here, at the head of the glen.

The *Life of Nectan* names Juliana as one of the daughters of Brychan, and a chapel set high on the rocky headland of Tintagel was dedicated to Juliana or rather to Juliet, a diminutive version of the name Juliana. In the sixth century, Tintagel was a

111. Site of the chapel, Nectan's Kieve.

chieftain's stronghold. It may have been occupied for only a few months each year, since Celtic rulers moved around their kingdoms, but we can guess that they lived in comfort at Tintagel from the unusual array of artefacts that have been excavated there: part of a huge wine container from the Aegean and a great oil jar from Tunisia; pieces of bowls from western Turkey, and a glass flagon from southern Spain. Some red dishes from Asia Minor were stamped with a cross, and were probably designed for use in worship.

Near the top of the fortress are the remains of Juliet's chapel. It was built in about 1000, and the east end was added around 1230, when a medieval castle was built on the site. The chapel's Norman font can now be seen in the parish church of St Materiana, on the mainland below the fortress. This church is set within what was perhaps the royal burial ground for the chieftains who lived in the fort above.[3]

From the sixth century until the twelfth, the fortress of Tintagel was abandoned; Juliet's chapel, however, remained in use. Unexpectedly, there are three wells on the rocky outcrop: a supply of fresh water was vital for a fort. Two of the wells are just beyond Juliet's ruined chapel; since they are fenced in, they can be easily spotted. There is a magnificent view from the chapel along the coast in both directions.

112. Juliet's chapel, Tintagel.

Another of her dedications is the church of St Juliot, in a remote valley 4 miles north-east of Tintagel. It can best be found by driving to Boscastle. You can then walk up the valley towards her church, or approach it by driving along a farm track from the opposite direction. Near the track, in a field below the church, is Juliet's holy well, although its surrounding stonework no longer survives. In 1894 the antiquarian Quiller-Couch observed stone carvings at the well, including a statue of the Virgin Mary. Pilgrims visited the spring, whose water was held to cure skin diseases.[4]

Surrounding the simple medieval church are three sturdy Celtic crosses (see overleaf). Cornish crosses are difficult to date, because they were carved in the same style for centuries. Some were preaching crosses, erected before a church was built; others commemorate an important person in the community. Some demarcated territorial boundaries, and others were set up as signposts or way-markers across the moors, to help travellers and pilgrims keep to the ancient paths and so find their way to the next settlement.

Churchyards often contain a number of crosses, but we cannot be sure that they are in their original location. Over the centuries, people brought them into churchyards,

113. Churchyard cross at St Juliot, near Boscastle.

114. Cross beside Juliet's church, Lanteglos.

either for safe-keeping or because the church was considered a holy place. Most Cornish crosses are constructed from hard local granite. Some, like that in the photograph, are neatly trimmed and carved. Others are so large and rough that they are likely to have been ancient standing stones, later Christianised by the addition of a cross.

Another church honours Juliet at Lanteglos-by-Camelford, 4 miles south-east of Tintagel. It was built beside a tributary of the River Allen. Nearby Camelford later became the centre of population, but Lanteglos was its mother church. The large, airy building dates from the fifteenth century, and a number of early crosses have been brought to its churchyard. Outside the church, a grave marker was erected by two Saxons for their father. It reads: 'Aelseth and Genereth wrought this family pillar for Aelwyne's soul and for themselves.' A nearby well is named after Juliet.

The author of the *Life of Nectan* was familiar with north Cornwall, for his list of Brychan's children includes a number of men or, more frequently, women, to whom north Cornish churches are dedicated. Cornish villages said to be named after the daughters of Brychan include St Juliot, St Wenn, St Endellion, St Teath, St Minver, St Mabyn and St Issey. Egloskerry (Church of Keri) and St Clether feature the names of Brychan's sons.

Since most of these saints' names differ from those in Welsh lists of Brychan's children, it appears that many of these saints and their stories are local to Cornwall. Nevertheless, some of their churches date back to ancient times. St Endellion church, for example, is built beside an early British cemetery.[5] However, since there are no written records from this time, we know little about the lives of these north Cornish saints.

St Clether is a village on the edge of Bodmin Moor, 10 miles south-east of Tintagel. The settlement is on a valley slope above the River Inney. Clether is listed in the *Life of Nectan* as one of Brychan's sons, and he is also mentioned in Welsh traditions. Brychan had a chaplain or soul-friend named Brynach, and a twelfth-century *Life of Brynach* describes a chieftain in Pembrokeshire named Clether, who had twenty sons and offered them to Brynach as servants. The 'righteous old man' then went to Cornwall, where he served God until his death.[6]

St Clether's chapel is built into the rocky hillside, a little below a solid well-house constructed over a spring. Its water flows down into the chapel, past three massive granite slabs which form its altar. The Normans built a church higher up the valley, but repaired the chapel and well, continuing to use it for baptisms. This entailed half a mile's walk through rough pasture and yellow gorse.

115. St Clether's well and chapel.

Clether's shrine was much visited by medieval pilgrims. In the fifteenth century, the building was altered: an oblong cavity was made in the east wall beside the altar, so that Clether's relics could be housed for veneration. The floor was lowered so that the water could flow out through the chapel into a second pool. A shelf for pilgrims' offerings was constructed above the pool. Behind the shelf was a small wooden door, which enabled a priest inside the building to retrieve the offerings. With these ingenious facilities, St Clether is the most complete medieval Cornish well and chapel.[7] It was restored in 1895. Today it is peaceful once again, surrounded by daffodils in springtime, as the River Inney winds through the valley below.

St Keyne (pronounced 'Cane') is a village near the south Cornish coast, 2 miles south of Liskeard. Keyne is described as one of the daughters of Brychan in twelfth-century Welsh genealogies, and a number of Welsh settlements are named after her. According to her legendary *Life*, she refused marriage and became a nun. She left Wales and crossed the River Severn in search of solitude. She lived for a while at a place infested by serpents, which she turned into stone. This was probably Keynsham, 4 miles south-east of Bristol, a settlement at a crossing-point of the River Avon. Ammonites, which are fossils shaped like coiled serpents, were found here, and may have given rise to the legend.[8] A similar miracle is attributed to Hilda of Whitby, where ammonites also abound.

116. St Keyne holy well.

Keyne continued to Cornwall, where she built many chapels; she was said to be wise and beautiful. She met Cadoc (see Chapter Nine) while he was on a pilgrimage to St Michael's Mount. This feature of her story is borrowed from a twelfth-century *Life of Cadoc*; it therefore helps us to date her own *Life*. Devotion to Keyne flourished in the later Middle Ages. She became the patron saint of several Cornish churches, and her feast day was celebrated elsewhere.

Keyne's holy well is down a leafy lane, a mile south of the parish church of St Keyne. There used to be four holy trees above the well. These were described by various antiquarians. In 1602, Richard Carew wrote:

> Four trees of divers kinde,
> Withy, Oke, Elme and Ash,
> Make with their roots an archèd roofe,
> Whose floore this spring doth wash.

The trees died, and were replaced in the early eighteenth century. These trees have also gone. The well-house was restored in 1932.[9]

CHAPTER TWENTY-ONE

PETROC, A WELSH PRINCE

A lthough Petroc was one of Cornwall's most popular saints in medieval times, we know little about him. His name may mean 'little Peter'. The earliest *Life of Petroc* survives in Breton manuscripts, but it was probably written by a Cornish cleric, since the author was familiar with various locations in Cornwall that were associated with Petroc. The eleventh-century biographer tells us that Petroc was a Welsh prince who became a monk and went to Ireland to study with his companions. They decided to sail to western Britain, and landed at Padstow on the north Cornish coast.

117. Padstow harbour.

118. Medieval statue of Petroc, Padstow.

The town's name means 'Petroc's stow'; the church was believed to be the site of Petroc's burial. To the right of the altar in the late medieval church there is a carving of Petroc in a monk's habit. He is bearded, and holds a walking stick and a hand-bell with which to summon people to pray. He also holds a book of the gospels, for he preaches the Word of God. The statue was probably preserved from an earlier church on the site, where it might have stood in a niche above the church porch for people to see as they entered the building. Outside the porch is a tall Celtic cross.

At the mouth of the River Camel, Padstow was an important harbour in early times: a sheltered port of entry for sailors from Ireland and south Wales. The author of Petroc's *Life* knew that Petroc was not the first monk to be honoured at Padstow, for the town's earlier name was Landuvethnoc, which means 'church site of Wethenoc'. The biographer therefore describes Petroc being received hospitably in Padstow by a bishop named Wethenoc. The bishop handed over his living quarters to Petroc, but asked that the settlement might continue to be named after himself.[1]

In the late tenth century, Petroc's shrine with his staff and his bell were taken inland to Bodmin, perhaps because of Viking raids around the coast. Augustinian canons encouraged Bodmin's development as a centre for pilgrimage to Petroc's shrine. In the late twelfth century, a canon of Bodmin priory wrote a longer *Life of Petroc*, connecting him into Welsh traditions, and claiming that he was the uncle of St Cadoc. This second author filled out further details about Cornish people and places. He states that Petroc surrounded his lands with ditches, traces of which could still be seen. By now, Petroc's church at Bodmin owned much property south of Padstow. The cleric appears to seek validation for this from Petroc himself by claiming that the saint had demarcated the land by digging boundary ditches.[2]

The first *Life of Petroc* describes the saint appointing a deputy to take charge of his monastery in Padstow. Petroc then went with twelve companions to live in a wilderness nearby. In the later *Life*, the Bodmin canon adds further details: the wilderness was a tidal creek in the estuary of the River Camel, named Nansfonteyn, or 'valley with a spring'. Here, Petroc built a chapel and a mill. A mill was essential to provide bread for food and for the eucharist. Petroc lived on 'bread and water, with porridge on Sundays'. The author describes Petroc practising the austere life traditional among early Irish monks: he immerses himself in the creek up to his neck, chanting the psalms.

Nansfonteyn, also known as Little Petherick, became a settlement of Petroc's followers. Today, the creek is still a tranquil place (see overleaf). Petroc's church is built into the hillside; four pinnacles that decorate its tower were brought from a ruined chapel dedicated to St Cadoc, in nearby Harlyn Bay. A short walk along the tributary of the Camel leads to Petroc's well, in a garden to the left of the track. The spring's course has altered: the water now tumbles past the dry well-house, which is half-covered with ivy. The path continues up into the woods that cover the hillside.

The writer of the first *Life of Petroc* describes a wealthy man named Constantine hunting deer at Little Petherick. Petroc interrupted the hunt, saved the stag and converted Constantine and his warriors to the Christian faith. The author was weaving local traditions into his story, for on the coast 3 miles north-west of Little Petherick lay St Constantine's chapel and holy well. The saint was believed to have been a converted chieftain. Over time his well-house was buried beneath sand dunes; it was rediscovered and excavated in 1911. It can be seen, carefully protected beneath a shelter, on the golf course in Constantine Bay.[3]

Petroc's second biographer describes how he continued inland with his companions to a more remote location, where a hermit named Guron lived. The writer is describing his own priory of Bodmin. At this time it may have been named Dinnurrin (meaning *dún* or fort of Uuron). Dinnurrin was the seat of the only known bishop of ninth-century Cornwall. Guron is more likely to have been a chieftain than a hermit, but medieval tradition incorporated him into Petroc's story.[4] The biographer describes how Guron welcomed Petroc and his three companions hospitably, setting out a table with white bread for them. Like Wethenoc earlier in the story, he left them his hut, and travelled a day's journey to Gorran near the Cornish coast, 7 miles south of St Austell. This village was the centre of Guron's cult.

119. Little Petherick Creek.

120. Guron's well, Bodmin.

Dwarfed by the splendid minster church of Bodmin is the hermit's well, in a sixteenth-century well-house. Above its entrance is a relief of Guron kneeling beneath a tree. He prays before a crucifix carved over the door of his cell. A great volume of water flows through pipes into a trough beside the main street, below the well.[5] Petroc's biographer relates that he too retired as a hermit, but while his predecessor, Guron, travelled southwards to the coast, Petroc journeyed northwards to the bleak open spaces of Bodmin Moor.

Petroc's shrine was in Bodmin church. In 1478 William Worcester visited it and wrote that Petroc's body rested in a beautiful shrine facing the Lady Chapel, at the east end of the church. His head-reliquary survives: it was fashioned by Arab craftsmen in Sicily in the twelfth century. It is a small, house-shaped casket made of ivory plates bound with brass strips, decorated with delicately carved medallions. The casket has been stolen twice. Martin, one of the canons, took it to the abbey of St Méen in Brittany in 1177, but it was traced and recovered. It was stolen once again in recent times, but is once more on view in the church.[6]

121. Petroc's church, Timberscombe.

At least eight Cornish churches, chapels and wells are dedicated to Petroc, and he was even more popular beyond Cornwall. Bodmin is not far from the Cornish border, and the Saxon kings seem to have encouraged the veneration of regional saints like St Swithin at Winchester and St Edmund at Bury St Edmunds. Religious, and therefore political, unity was strengthened when pilgrims travelled with a common purpose from one part of Britain to another. Petroc's feast day is listed in various cathedral calendars, and relics of Petroc were venerated in many of them.

Close to the north Somerset coast, Timberscombe acquired Petroc as its patron saint. It is one of a group of churches dedicated to early Welsh monks: nearby Carhampton is named after Carantoc; Porlock honours Dubricius, and a church and holy well outside Watchet are dedicated to Decuman. The north Somerset coast was an easy day's sail from south Wales, across the sheltered waters of the Bristol Channel.

Timberscombe is one of several churches in this area with a magnificent rood screen. This is a wooden screen, once topped with a cross, or rood; it separated the priest in the chancel from the congregation, who stood in the nave. Wood was plentiful in the area, and there were skilled carvers at Dunster abbey. The photograph opposite shows the middle portion of Timberscombe's screen, with its imitation stone

122. Church porch, Llanbedr-y-cennin.

tracery, columns and fan vaulting. St Petroc's church also contains a wall painting of King David chanting psalms while playing the harp, and medieval floor tiles brought from nearby Cleeve abbey.

There are a number of churches dedicated to Petroc in Wales, and local Welsh traditions about the saint are quite different from Cornish ones. There is a church of Llanbedrog ('church of Petroc') in Verwick, near the coastal town of Ceredigion. A fifteenth-century Welshman wrote a poem praying for Petroc's help in driving away sand dunes that were threatening Verwick. Celtic saints were generally held in greater honour if they were born elsewhere, so the Welsh poet claims that Petroc came from an ancient line of Cornish kings, in the same way that Petroc's Cornish biographer gives him a royal Welsh lineage.[7]

In the poem, Petroc is described as one of seven Britons who fought alongside King Arthur, and escaped alive from his last fatal battle. Petroc had a famous spear, which he laid aside after Arthur's defeat. He became a monk, arrived in Verwick, and later died there. A Welsh manuscript from around 1510 calls him 'Petroc Splinter-Spear'. In 1535, Llanbedrog church in north Wales claimed to possess the very spear! Pilgrims came and made offerings when they saw it.[8]

Llanbedr-y-cennin means 'church of Peter among the leeks' (see previous page). The village may be dedicated to Petroc; it is situated on the western valley slope above the Conwy River, 5 miles south of the town and castle of Conwy. It is a single-chambered early medieval church that was enlarged by the addition of a new chancel in the fifteenth century. In the sixteenth, a fine timbered porch was built, with a flagstone floor. The small church still contains its eighteenth-century box pews, where each family sat in privacy to listen to the preacher.

CHAPTER TWENTY-TWO

LOCAL CORNISH SAINTS

ST MADERN

The village of Madron is in the moorland, a mile north-west of Penzance, in the far west of the country. It contains one of Cornwall's oldest and most famous holy wells. The settlement is dedicated to Madern, about whom nothing is known. He may have been unique to this village, where people were named after him; even today, Maddern is a common surname in the area. Madron church was an ancient one: a pre-Christian standing stone now in the church was re-used in the sixth or seventh century to mark a Christian burial.[1] In time, Madron became the mother church of Penzance.

St Madern's well (see overleaf) is a mile north of the church, along a clearly signed, muddy track. It is set in a grove of ancient sallow willows, and bubbles up through marshy ground. Hung on the branches are hundreds of clouties, or strips of cloth: these are symbolic prayers for healing or in gratitude for a cure. This ancient custom is seen at some other wells in Britain and Ireland, and is also found across Europe, Asia, Africa and South America.[2]

Madern's chapel with its baptistery is 75 metres further along the track. There are the foundations of a solid twelfth-century building with a granite altar and a baptismal basin built into its north-west corner. It was partially demolished at the time of the Reformation, and seventeenth-century observers noted a great thorn tree, whose branches formed a leafy roof over the chapel. Each year, parishioners used turf to repair a green bank alongside the altar, which they called 'St Madern's Bed'. Sick people came to bathe in the well and sleep on the bed, and many of them were cured, including a cripple who recovered so completely that he later enlisted in the army and was killed in action in 1644.[3]

123. Tree with clouties, Madron well.

ST SELEVAN

The hamlet of St Levan is 3 miles south-east of Land's End; it overlooks the sea, which turns turquoise and azure as it pounds the white shingle of Porthgwarra Cove. The church is set in a sheltered hollow above the cliffs; it is dedicated to Selevan, whose name comes from that of King Solomon. The Irish surname Sullivan is another form of Solomon. Celtic Christians liked to have biblical characters as their patrons: we have already met monks named after Samson (Chapter Nineteen), the prophet Daniel (Chapter Thirteen), King David (Chapter Eight) and his cantor, Asaph (Chapter Sixteen).

Selevan may have been the son of a Cornish chieftain named Gereint, and the father of Cybi, who has dedications in both Cornwall and Wales. Stories recorded at St Levan in the eighteenth century describe Selevan as a hermit and fisherman. His church was built beside a pre-Christian holy stone: a large fissured rock in the churchyard. Perhaps to counteract its power, six tall, elegant Celtic crosses were erected, three at either door of the church. One still stands, almost 3 metres tall, and the heads of two others can be seen in the churchyard.

Across the road, a track leads down to Selevan's baptistery, above the cove. This is a small square building, constructed of giant slabs; it was roofed until the eighteenth

124. Selevan's baptistery, Porthgwarra Cove.

century. Adjoining it is Selevan's holy well, which was known for curing eye diseases and toothache.[4] People bathed in the well, and then slept on the stone floor of the baptistery. Further down the path to the cove, a hermit's two-roomed chapel and cell can be seen, also edged with granite boulders. Excavation revealed a roughly flagged stone floor. It was a sheltered spot for a hermit, with easy fishing in the cove below.

ST PAUL AURELIAN

The parish of Paul is near the coast, 2 miles south of Penzance. It is probably named after Paul Aurelian, a prominent figure in Celtic times. The shortest crossing to Brittany is from this part of Cornwall, and Paul's *Life* was written in 884 at the Breton monastery of Landévennec. The biographer conflated his story with that of one or possibly two other Pauls, but it seems that Paul Aurelian was born in Wales into an important Romano-British family in the late fifth century. The author tells us that as a young man, Paul studied alongside David and Samson in Illtud's famous monastery at Llanilltud Fawr.

According to his biographer, Paul left Illtud's community at the age of sixteen and became a hermit. In time, his fame reached the court of King Mark, also known as Cunomorus, who may have lived in the hill-fort of Castle Dore, near Fowey (see

125. Celtic cross, Paul churchyard.

Chapter Nineteen). Mark ruled over peoples who spoke four languages, and wished to strengthen their Christian faith. At his invitation, Paul arrived with twelve priests. He spent some time working there, but when he was asked to become a bishop, he left and sailed to Brittany.[5]

Paul founded a church on the Île-de-Batz, and agreed to become the first bishop of the settlement which was later named St-Pol-de-Léon in his honour. He was widely venerated in this area of Brittany. We do not know whether Paul Aurelian worked in the Cornish parish named after him, or whether it was given its name later by Breton monks who brought his cult to Cornwall. The church is at an ancient holy site, for built into the churchyard wall is a Neolithic standing stone, perhaps 4,000 years old, capped with a Celtic cross. It stands beside the old road leading down to Mousehole harbour, which was an embarkation point for Brittany in early times.

ST SIDWELL

The biographer of Paul Aurelian tells us that he had a sister named Sitofolla, a nun who lived near the sea-shore. She may be the saint named Sidwell who is honoured at Laneast, a village on the north-eastern edge of Bodmin Moor. Sidwell's cult-centre was

126. Laneast holy well.

in Exeter, where she had a church and a holy well. We first hear of Sidwell in the late Anglo-Saxon period, and people came to her shrine for healing throughout medieval times. Her name was given to girls in many parts of Devon and Cornwall, particularly in the sixteenth and seventeenth centuries.[6]

In the twelfth century, the bishop of Exeter compiled a book of liturgical readings for use in the cathedral, in which he records Sidwell's story as it was then told: her stepmother had her murdered by labourers reaping in the fields, who cut off her head with their scythes. This preserves a pre-Christian myth, in which the harvest goddess was said to die when reapers cut the last sheaf of corn. This was ritually enacted on farms throughout the Middle Ages, and into recent times. In some places, each reaper in turn threw his sickle at the last sheaf, so that no one could be held responsible for killing the spirit of the corn. Sometimes they performed a ceremony called 'crying the neck', when they honoured the last sheaf, or neck, of corn, in which the corn spirit was now seen to reside.[7]

Sidwell is depicted with her scythe on rood screens, bench ends and windows in about twenty churches in the south-west. It is not known when Laneast was dedicated to her. A tall Celtic cross stands near the church porch. Her holy well is 300 metres south-east of the church, along a signed track through a field. It has a fine sixteenth-century granite well-house (see p. 171); its water flows downhill to join the River Inney. It was formerly used for christenings, and is also known as Jordan Well, to recall the baptism of Jesus.[8] For the same reason, church fonts were sometimes called Jordans.

ST CUBERT

We know little about Cubert, who gave his name to a village south of Newquay, a mile from the sea. A farm named Lanlovey next to Cubert church suggests that this was a Celtic foundation, since the prefix *lan* is the Celtic word for a church site. An inscribed gravestone set into the outer wall of the tower indicates an early Christian cemetery here. Cubert may have been the Welsh saint who gave his name to Gwbert-on-Sea, 2 miles north of Ceredigion.[9] The Welsh village is only a mile from Verwick, where people prayed to Petroc to save them from the encroaching sand dunes (see Chapter Twenty-one).

In his Cornish parish, Cubert is honoured at a freshwater well in a sea cave, beyond the sand dunes in Holywell Bay. There are three caves, and in the furthest of these, a series of steps against the cave wall leads up to four or five shallow pools, formed by condensation dripping from the cave roof. The rock is pink and white from calcareous deposits, and the cave is accessible for only an hour each day, at low tide. In wet weather, the rocks are too slippery to climb, but in dryer conditions, one can clamber past the pools into a chamber in the cave roof.

127. Cubert's well, Holywell Bay.

In earlier times, pilgrims flocked to the well, which was good for bowel conditions and cured children's diseases. Mothers brought sick or deformed children here, dipping them into the pools, and taking them into the inner chamber. Cripples left their crutches here. By the fourteenth century, the parish was considered to honour the northern saint, Cuthbert (see Chapter Twenty-four), but thirteenth-century documents name the parish saint as Cubert.[10]

ST RUMON

Ruan Lanihorne is a settlement beside an arm of the River Fal, 4 miles south-east of Truro. Its name means 'Rumon's *lan* (or church site) on the promontory'. This small village was a flourishing market town with a harbour until the seventeenth century. Its medieval castle was demolished in 1718. Near the church, an old road leads down to the River Fal. Settlements in the Fal estuary were busy in earlier times: here, ships could penetrate into the heart of Cornwall, and monks in monasteries near the tidal river could easily sail to Brittany.[11]

128. Ruan Lanihorne well.

Rumon's well is in a very boggy wood below the church. Old engravings show its fine arched well-house, with its masonry already split open by trees. This was once the middle of the village. The spring water pours out through a chute, opposite a duck pond. We know little about Rumon, whose name is a form of the Latin name, Romanus. Ruan Lanihorne was probably the site of his shrine until the tenth or eleventh century, when most of his relics were taken to Tavistock abbey in south Devon. Romansleigh in north Devon may be named after Rumon; it belonged to Tavistock abbey.

William of Malmesbury visited Tavistock abbey in 1120 and saw the effigy of Rumon 'buried as a bishop, decorated with a beautiful shrine'. Later, a monk of Tavistock wrote a *Life of Rumon*, adapting the story of a different Rumon, who lived in Brittany. By the mid-thirteenth century, relics of Rumon were kept at Glastonbury abbey, where he was described as a bishop, and a brother of the Welsh and Breton saint Tudwal. Although little is known about him, Rumon was a popular saint. On the Lizard, a holy well and the two villages of Ruan Major and Ruan Minor are dedicated to him, and two men named after him appear in the late Anglo-Saxon *Bodmin Gospels*. Rumon was still honoured at Ruan Lanihorne in 1525, when a woman named Marion Lelley left a cow in her will to the church property store of St Rumon.[12]

PART V

NORTHUMBRIA AND
THE ISLE OF MAN

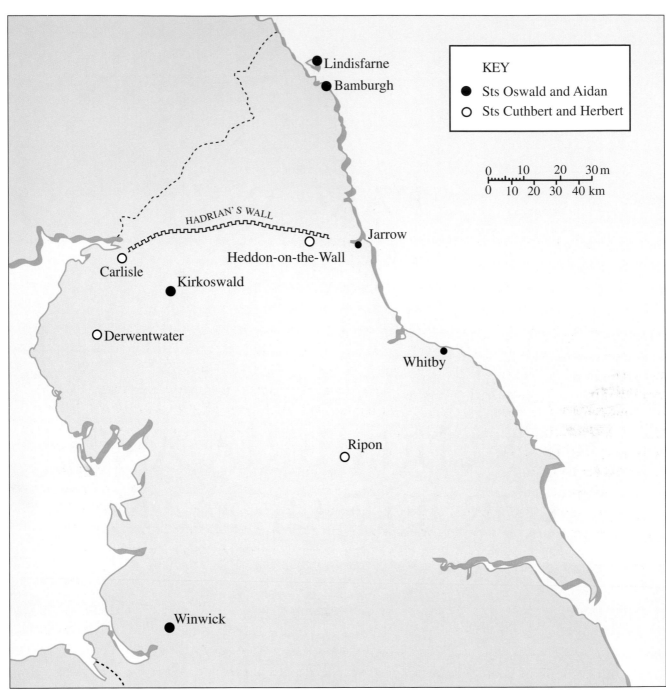

KEY

● Sts Oswald and Aidan
○ Sts Cuthbert and Herbert

Lindisfarne

Bamburgh

HADRIAN'S WALL

Jarrow

Heddon-on-the-Wall

Carlisle

Kirkoswald

Derwentwater

Whitby

Ripon

Winwick

Map 5: Saints of Northumbria

CHAPTER TWENTY-THREE

AĬÐAN AND KĬNG OSWALÐ

Oswald (604–42) was perhaps Britain's most renowned royal soldier saint. He was a Saxon, a son of King Ethelfrith of Northumbria. When the King's brother Edwin seized the kingdom in 616, his two sons fled to Iona (see Chapter Seventeen), where they were educated by the monks. Seventeen years later, after Edwin's death, the family returned to Northumbria. Oswald's brother was killed by the British king, Cadwallon, who then occupied Northumbria, but Oswald defeated Cadwallon in battle at Heavenfield, near Hexham, beside Hadrian's Wall. After his training on Iona, Oswald was a devout Christian, although most of his army were probably still pagan. Oswald gathered his soldiers round a wooden cross to pray for victory and, although heavily outnumbered, he won the battle. Now aged thirty, Oswald became King of Northumbria, and united its two regions of Bernicia and Deira. He married the daughter of the king of Wessex, and other Anglo-Saxon kings acknowledged him as their overlord. Since Oswald wished his people to become Christian, he sent to Iona for a bishop to convert his subjects.

Our chief source of information about the spread of Christianity in Northumbria is Bede's *Ecclesiastical History of the English Nation*. Bede spent most of his life in the monastery of Jarrow, which is beside the River Tyne, east of Newcastle. He wrote his great book in about 731, a hundred years after Oswald's reign. When he described events in Northumbria, he was able to draw on the knowledge of elderly monks in his own community. Bede tells us: 'When King Oswald asked for a Scottish bishop to preach the gospel to himself and his people, first (Colmán) was sent, an austere man who was unsuccessful. The English people ignored him, so he returned home, and reported to the assembled council that he had been unable to do any good among the people to whom he was sent to preach. They were uncivilised, stubborn and barbarous.'[1] The monks gathered on Iona discussed what to do, and an Irishman named Aidan suggested that Colmán might have been too severe. The community therefore decided to consecrate Aidan as bishop, and sent him to Northumbria in place of Colmán.

Aidan arrived in Northumbria with twelve companions in 635. Bede describes Aidan with affection and admiration. He did not approve of the Irish bishop's method of

129. Oswald's well, Kirkoswald.

calculating Easter, but he praised his love of prayer and study, his gentleness and humility, and his care for the sick and the poor. It is possible that Bede's unusually lavish words were intended as a reproof for the lax bishops of his own time. Bede relates: 'When (Aidan) arrived, at his request the king gave him the island of Lindisfarne for his bishop's seat. Here the tide ebbs and flows twice a day, so the place is surrounded by the sea and becomes an island. Again twice a day, the shore becomes dry and is joined to the land. . . . The bishop was not skilled at speaking English, and when he preached the gospel, it was most delightful to see the king himself interpreting God's word to his commanders and ministers, for he had learnt to speak fluent Gaelic during his lengthy exile.'[2]

Aidan and Oswald travelled long distances together. West of the Pennines, both men are commemorated in the Eden valley at the village of Kirkoswald, 8 miles north of Penrith. Here they are said to have found the people worshipping the spirit of a spring. They built a church over the spring, whose water flows under the nave and emerges outside the west wall of the church, where it can be drunk from a well.

King Oswald lived in a fortress on a rocky outcrop at Bamburgh, 15 miles south-east of Berwick-upon-Tweed. There may have been a coastal fort on this site in Roman and pre-Roman times. In 547 the Anglian King Ida fought his way northwards to become the first king of Northumbria. He seized the fortress and made it his capital. It is an ideal defensive site, commanding a view of attackers from either land or sea. Three hundred years after Oswald's time, the fortress was captured by King Athelstan of Wessex, the grandson of Alfred the Great, when he was conquering England and Scotland. It was subsequently raided by Vikings, who destroyed it in 993. However the Normans, too, found it a useful stronghold: in 1157 King Henry II built the great keep at the centre of the castle.

From Oswald's fortress, Aidan's island monastery of Lindisfarne was just visible, 6 miles up the coast. Bede says of Aidan: 'When he was invited to eat with the king, which was not often, he went with one or two monks. After eating frugally, he left as soon as possible, in order to read (the scriptures) or write.'[3] On one occasion, after Aidan had celebrated the Easter Vigil with his community, he was invited to join the royal household for dinner. Bede relates that a silver dish of food was put before Aidan and Oswald, 'and they were about to say grace, when suddenly the servant entered who was responsible for feeding the poor. He told the king that a large number of beggars had come from everywhere. They were sitting in the streets, begging alms from the king. At once he ordered the food to be taken to the poor, and the dish to be cut up and also given to them.'[4]

Oswald ruled for only eight years. At the age of thirty-eight, he was killed in battle by the pagan King Penda of Mercia at Maserfield. This was probably near Oswestry, in Shropshire. Penda ordered his soldiers to mutilate Oswald's body: his head, arms and hands were hung on stakes. Oswestry's name derives from 'Oswald's tree', following a legend that Penda hung him from a tree in mock crucifixion.

The saint's holy well can be found a few streets from the parish church, in Oswald Place. At one time there was a stone carving of the king's head here, and it was believed that his head was buried at the well. There was once an oratory above the spring, for in the 1530s the antiquarian John Leland wrote: 'There is a chapel over it of timber, and the fountain environed with a stone wall.'[5] Springs become resting places for severed heads in other Celtic legends, and royal heads were considered to be particularly potent. Throughout the centuries, people have symbolically continued this custom by throwing into wells coins displaying a monarch's head.

130. Oswald's well, Oswestry.

Oswald was soon regarded as one of Britain's national heroes. The Saxons admired his bravery and military skill, his faith and generosity and his early death while fighting for his people. Sixty-two churches were dedicated to him in England, and many more in Europe. Oswald was commemorated in most English calendars, and many places claimed his relics. St Oswald's church at Winwick in Lancashire was close to the lowest crossing point of the River Mersey. Oswald's army would have travelled west from Bamburgh, then down England's west coast, crossing the Mersey at Winwick Quay as they marched south to fight King Penda at Maserfield. They would have returned northwards through Winwick after the death of their king.

The present church, in its large, raised churchyard, dates from the fourteenth century. Inside are the arms of an elaborate tenth-century wheel cross. One of its end panels depicts two of Penda's soldiers dismembering Oswald. They look sinister as they trample on the king's head, while severing his legs from his body. The other end panel of the cross appears to depict a priest carrying a bucket of water from Oswald's nearby well. In the background is the parish church and its preaching cross. Seen in the photograph are wooden copies of the two panels from the cross.

The hamlet of Hermitage Green, a mile and a half north of Winwick, is one of several places claimed to be the site of Oswald's death. Bede wrote that the place where Oswald died was the scene of many miracles of healing, and that a depression was made in the ground by people removing soil, in order to heal their sick. Bede

131. Oswald's martyrdom, from Winwick cross.

wrote: 'as the earth was gradually removed, a pit was left in which a man could stand.'[6] This was said to be the origin of St Oswald's well in Hermitage Green. It is in a field above the hamlet, across the road from Monk House. In the village below, an eighteenth-century inn is named The Hermit. Both names refer to the hermit monk who tended the well.

Oswald was succeeded as king by his cousin, Oswin. Bede thought highly of the new king, and described him as 'friendly in speech and courteous in behaviour. He was very generous, to the noble and ignoble alike. Everyone loved him for his physical and mental gifts. From almost every province, people of the highest rank came to serve him. Among his gifts and unusual graces, if I may say so, he was said to be extraordinarily humble.'[7] Bede describes an emotional meal shortly before Oswin's death. Aidan attended the banquet, having recently given away to a beggar a very fine horse which he had received from Oswin. The king came into the feast straight from a hunting trip, and chided Aidan for his generosity to the beggar. He went over to the fire with his attendants, to warm himself, and then returned to Aidan to apologise. In the course of the meal, Aidan felt a premonition of Oswin's approaching death. He wept, and turning to the monk who was with him, he explained in Gaelic the reason for his sadness. The rest of the company did not understand what he said. Soon afterwards, Oswin was treacherously slain by his cousin, Oswy. Bede adds that Aidan was to die only twelve days later.[8]

132. Oswald's well, Hermitage Green.

Bede tells us how Bishop Aidan lived: he liked to travel on foot rather than on horseback, and engaged people in conversation. If they were pagan, he taught them about Christianity; if they were believers, he encouraged them. He taught those around him, both monks and lay-people, to read the gospels and to learn the psalms. When he received money, he gave it to the poor, or used it to ransom Anglo-Saxon slaves, many of whom he educated and ordained as priests.[9] He owned a church and a few surrounding fields outside the fortress at Bamburgh, and from here he went on preaching expeditions, staying at Oswald's residences in other parts of his kingdom.[10] This appears to have been quite an itinerant way of life; Bede does not tell us how much time Aidan spent with his community on Lindisfarne.

133. Medieval squint, Bamburgh church.

We learn that Aidan spent each Lent on the Farne Islands, about 2 miles offshore, for an extended period of solitude. He was on Farne when King Penda ravaged Northumbria and reached the royal stronghold at Bamburgh. His soldiers set fire to the fortress, and Aidan, seeing the flames from his cell on Farne, prayed until the wind changed direction and the flames engulfed Penda's troops, who were forced to retreat.[11]

Aidan became ill while in his church at Bamburgh. His followers built a shelter for him beside the church, and Aidan died while resting against a wooden beam for support. The plank survived when Penda burnt the church; it is still preserved. The impressive church that exists today was built between 1170 and 1230 by a community of Augustinian canons. Its chancel is probably on the site of Aidan's church.[12] The photograph illustrates the fourteenth-century squint that enabled those in the nave to watch the priest at the altar. Aidan's monks took his body back to Lindisfarne for burial. During his sixteen years as bishop, much of Northumbria had become Christian, largely as a result of Aidan's dedicated work.

CHAPTER TWENTY-FOUR

CUThBERT, BiShop of LINDiSFARNE

L ike Oswald, Cuthbert (*c.* 634–87) was an Anglo-Saxon who was trained by Celtic monks. He lived a generation after Oswald, and once more, Bede tells us much about Cuthbert, drawing on information from monks who knew him. In 638 the Angles of Northumbria advanced into Scotland, where they held territory for almost fifty years. During this time, Bishop Aidan sent monks from Lindisfarne to establish a community at Melrose in the Scottish Borders, at a bend in the River Tweed (see map 3). An old monk named Sigfrid from Bede's own monastery of Jarrow had been a novice at Melrose, and could remember the day when a youth named Cuthbert rode up to the enclosure gate at Melrose and leapt down from his horse. He handed its bridle to a servant, together with his spear, in order to enter the church and pray. The prior, named Boisil, was standing at the monastery door and noted young Cuthbert with approval. He asked why the youth had come, and the eighteen-year-old replied that he would prefer life in the monastery to life in the world. Boisil welcomed Cuthbert kindly, told the abbot, and received permission for Cuthbert to have his head shorn and be enrolled among the brothers.[1]

Sigfrid recalled that the teenage Cuthbert was outstanding at study, work and prayer. He avoided wine and beer, but ate heartily because he was strong and well-built. Boisil took the young monk with him on preaching expeditions for a week or a month at a time. They travelled on horseback or on foot, often visiting remote settlements in mountainous areas that no monks had previously visited. Boisil offered Cuthbert a model of evangelisation that the younger monk was to adopt for the rest of his life. After Boisil's death, Cuthbert continued his missionary journeys, accompanied by one or two brothers. He sailed to the kingdom of Fife on the Scottish east coast: Bede notes that he made this expedition during a mild winter and arrived the day after Christmas. Cuthbert was taken off guard when the weather became severe, and his little group was plagued by cold and hunger.[2]

Cuthbert travelled even further north to evangelise the Picts around Loch Tay. Between Aberfeldy and the loch, there was a Pictish monastery at a place named Dull that a number of Lindisfarne monks appear to have used as a base, since there are

134. Cuthbert's pool at Weem, near Aberfeldy.

nearby dedications to Cuthbert, Cedd and possibly Chad. Two miles east of Dull is St Cuthbert's chapel at Weem (see map 3). As we saw in Chapter Eighteen, the name of the settlement means 'cave' (or *uaimh* in Gaelic). Cuthbert's chapel is in the valley of the River Tay, and cliffs rise steeply behind the little church. Cuthbert's cave is a hollow in the rock; nearby, water dripping from the cliff face gathers in a small pool, seen in the photograph above. According to his Irish *Life*, Cuthbert built an oratory here and drank from the pool. It is now named St David's well, after a fifteenth-century local laird who lived beside it as a hermit. The chapel below contains two sturdy crosses from the nearby Pictish monastery; a third is still in place at Dull.[3]

In about 659, King Alcfrith gave the abbot of Melrose a tract of land on which to build a monastery at Ripon in north Yorkshire, 120 miles south of Melrose. The abbot, named Eata, selected a group of monks to travel south with him to Ripon, and asked Boisil to replace him as abbot of Melrose. Eata chose Cuthbert, now aged twenty-five, to go to Ripon as its guestmaster. However, the community stayed in Ripon only two years before being ousted by Wilfred, an ambitious monk who had trained at Lindisfarne and later studied in Rome. Wilfred enjoyed royal patronage, and the king appointed him as abbot in place of Eata.

Wilfred introduced the Benedictine rule, and built a new stone church with an impressive crypt which perhaps housed the relics of saints that Wilfred brought back from Rome, intending to install them in the new churches that he planned to build. There are cressets for oil lamps in the walls of the crypt. One of its narrow chambers can be seen in the photograph. Wilfred built a similar crypt at Hexham, near Hadrian's Wall; it, too, survives intact. Wilfred's church at Ripon was dedicated in 672; later, when monks from Lindisfarne were fleeing from the Vikings, bearing Cuthbert's body, they stopped for a while at Ripon, before eventually settling at Durham. Vikings also destroyed Wilfred's church at Ripon, apart from its crypt. It was later rebuilt by the Normans.

135. Wilfred's crypt in Ripon Cathedral.

Eata, Cuthbert and the Celtic monks returned to Melrose. Three years later, plague struck the community. Both Cuthbert and Boisil were infected. Bede tells us that Cuthbert recovered, although his digestion was permanently affected. Boisil sensed that he would soon die, and suggested to Cuthbert that for their remaining time together they might study St John's Gospel. Boisil continued: '"I have a copy consisting of seven quarto sheets. With God's help, we can read one every day, and meditate on it as far as we are able." They did this, and speedily accomplished the task, for they tried to read with simple faith that works through love, and did not burden themselves with subtleties or minute questions. After their seven days of study, Boisil died.'[4]

Eata became abbot of Lindisfarne in 664, and brought Cuthbert with him as prior. Eata came to a troubled community. The Council of Whitby had recently take place; it had been convened by the king to decide whether Northumbria should follow Celtic or Roman customs. The main debate took place between Wilfred and Colmán, the abbot of Lindisfarne. The king favoured the Irish position, but was compelled by Wilfred's arguments. The debate was concluded, and Colmán resigned as abbot of Lindisfarne. He returned to Iona, taking with him most of the Celtic monks and thirty Anglo-Saxons. It was left to Eata and his young prior to rebuild the community on

Lindisfarne, to restore its shattered morale, and implement Roman customs peacefully. Cuthbert was an experienced monk, with patience and discretion. Bede describes his skill at mediation: 'In discussion with the brothers, when he was weary of the bitter taunts of those who opposed him, he would quietly rise from his seat and dismiss the meeting until the following day. Then he would use the same exhortations as before, as if he had not been attacked, until he brought them round to his own views. He showed remarkable patience.'[5]

Bede approved of Lindisfarne because, as he said, even though the island was small, the monastery was well organised, with the abbot, priests and deacons, singers and readers leading an ordered monastic life. As the first bishop of Lindisfarne, Aidan had set a model of living simply as one of the monks, and this tradition continued in Cuthbert's day. Bede describes Cuthbert busy praying, or making something with his hands, or walking round the island to inspect his property. He noted that Cuthbert used to celebrate Eucharist not in a loud voice, but quietly, often shedding tears. While he did not dress in a slovenly way, he preferred simple materials, and even in Bede's time the monks wore unbleached vestments of natural wool.[6] Some of Cuthbert's belongings were preserved by his brothers and were buried with him, including an ivory comb with a row of thick teeth along one edge and thin teeth along the other.[7]

Little survives on Lindisfarne from Cuthbert's day: the monastery was destroyed by Vikings in 793 and the monks left the island a generation later, dismantling their wooden church and taking its timbers with them.[8] The surviving priory ruins date from the twelfth century. The nearby parish church of St Mary may stand on the site of a second Anglo-Saxon one. South-west of the priory is a rocky islet which Cuthbert used as a retreat. At low tide it is ten minutes' walk from the priory, but at high tide it is cut off from the mainland. Seen in the photograph opposite are the remains of a medieval chapel on the island, its ruined walls covered with pink thrift and yellow birdsfoot trefoil. At its east end, a tall wooden cross marks the site of the altar. More fragmentary stones may be the remains of Cuthbert's hermitage.

After ten years as prior of Lindisfarne, Cuthbert went to live as a hermit on Inner Farne, following Aidan's example. However, while his predecessor spent only short periods on the island, Cuthbert remained on Farne for ten years, and constructed buildings to suit his needs. Bede describes these in some detail: a circular hut, taller than himself, with walls made of rough stones and turf dug from the floor. Its roof was constructed of poles thatched with straw. A second chamber formed Cuthbert's chapel. Further away, beside the landing stage, he built a large guest-house for visiting monks. He thatched its roof, although crows caused problems by pulling out straw in order to build their nests. Visitors could drink water from a nearby well. By digging, Cuthbert also discovered a spring in his own compound.[9] He asked the monks from Lindisfarne to bring him farm tools and wheat seed, which he planted in the springtime. When it failed to germinate, he tried barley, and this grew well.[10]

136. St Cuthbert's Isle, Lindisfarne.

At first when monks came to visit him, Cuthbert would leave his hermitage in order to make them welcome. He washed their feet in warm water, and Bede records that the monks in turn would persuade Cuthbert to have his feet washed also, for he became so used to seclusion that he often forgot to take off his leather gaiters for months, and sometimes removed his shoes only on Holy Thursday, when feet are ceremonially washed during the Lord's Supper. Over the years, however, Cuthbert stopped visiting his guests, and remained in his cell to pray.[11] Sometimes his visitors found themselves put on the spot. Bede describes how Cuthbert left his cell to give advice to some guests; he also told them to cook and eat a goose that was hanging on the wall, rather than sail away hungry. Presumably the goose had been brought by a previous visitor. The guests had sufficient provisions, however, and they decided to leave the bird for Cuthbert. A storm forced them to return to Farne, however, and Cuthbert made them boil the kettle and cook the goose![12]

After ten years, King Egfrith and Theodore, Archbishop of Canterbury, prevailed on Cuthbert to become bishop of Hexham. Cuthbert, aged fifty, agreed, but soon exchanged his diocese with that of Eata, and became responsible for Lindisfarne instead. He once more began to preach, teach and travel throughout his diocese.

He gave out food and clothing, and consecrated churches. Cuthbert journeyed back and forth along Hadrian's Wall to Carlisle. Here there was a double monastery, whose abbess was the sister of Queen Iurminburg. Bede describes the queen waiting apprehensively in her sister's monastery while her husband Egfrith fought his last fatal battle against the Picts in Scotland. Cuthbert prepared the queen to hear the news she dreaded.[13] As he travelled along Hadrian's Wall, he is said to have stopped to preach at Heddon-on-the-Wall, a settlement 8 miles west of Newcastle upon Tyne. The Roman wall can still be seen at Heddon; in the foreground of the photograph, a circular medieval kiln has been built into the ancient wall.

In 686 Cuthbert again visited Carlisle to ordain priests and to visit the queen. A hermit named Herbert also travelled to Carlisle to spend time with Cuthbert. Herbert lived on an island in Cumbria, on Derwentwater, which was then a marshy lake. Each year he used to travel 100 miles to Lindisfarne in order to visit Cuthbert. Since Carlisle was only 20 miles north of Derwentwater, Herbert took advantage of Cuthbert's visit for what proved to be their last encounter, since the two men were both to die on 20 March the following year. The photograph on p. 190 is taken from Friar's Crag on the lake-shore, a mile south of Keswick. From this point, monks set out to visit Herbert on his island, which is the further, fainter one. Remains of a circular stone building on the island may be his hermitage. The Derwent Fells rise steeply on the far side of the lake.

After only two years as bishop of Lindisfarne, Cuthbert returned to Inner Farne to die. Monks from Lindisfarne visited him regularly, but in the last week of his life violent storms prevented them from reaching Cuthbert for five days. Herefrid, Abbot of Lindisfarne, was Cuthbert's attendant, and told Bede the story of Cuthbert's death in considerable detail. On his arrival after the storm, he found that Cuthbert had collapsed in the guest-house by the landing stage. Herefrid warmed some water to wash Cuthbert's feet, for he had an ulcer on his leg. He also warmed some wine that he had brought, as since his collapse Cuthbert had managed to eat only a piece of raw onion. The abbot returned home, leaving two monks to care for Cuthbert. Herefrid returned frequently and, as Cuthbert weakened, the sick man asked to be carried to his chapel to die.

Herefrid described Cuthbert's final hours: 'I went in to him about the ninth hour and found him lying in the corner of his chapel, before the altar. I sat beside him but he spoke very little, for the burden of his suffering prevented him from speaking much.' The abbot asked Cuthbert for some final words to the community and Cuthbert spoke, little by little, as he found the strength to do so. Herefrid gave him the sacrament, and Cuthbert stretched out his hands in prayer, and then died. Herefrid went out to tell the waiting monks, one of whom lit two torches and climbed to a high point on the island, to signal to the brothers waiting on Lindisfarne that Cuthbert was dead. A monk was standing at a similar high spot on Lindisfarne and, seeing the signal, he ran to the monastery to tell the community.[14]

137. Medieval settlement at Heddon-on-the-Wall.

Cuthbert's body was taken back to Lindisfarne for burial. Eleven years later, the monks dug up his remains in order to enshrine them. His body was found to be undecayed and was placed in a carved oak casket. Lindisfarne was later devastated by Norsemen and the monks fled, taking Cuthbert's relics with them. After many years of wandering around northern Britain with the precious casket, the brothers selected Durham for its resting place. Fragments of the finely-carved shrine can still be seen in Durham Cathedral.

Map 6: The Isle of Man

CHAPTER TWENTY-FIVE

The Isle of Man

At the time when the Celtic churches were flourishing, the Isle of Man was a useful landing place for travellers between Ireland, Scotland and Wales. It was not the most direct route, but it provided safe harbours and fresh water, and successive peoples made use of the island as they sailed between the countries surrounding the Irish Sea.[1] Christianity probably reached the island by 500, and contact with Christian communities overseas brought literacy and new technological ideas. However, people's way of life was not greatly affected. Roman civilisation and culture had scarcely touched the island. No local pottery was made after the fifth century BC, and little domestic equipment has survived. Instead, organic materials such as leather, wood and stone were used for containers. Wheeled vehicles were not constructed on the island until recent times.

Irish families settled on the Isle of Man in early times, and some of them may have been Christian. Stone carvings suggest that Christians also came to the island from south Wales. The first consecrated burial grounds were established, and most of these were later served by a small chapel, or 'keeill' in Manx. Early Christian graves are often marked by numerous white quartz pebbles, which symbolised prayers for the dead. This was an ancient and widespread practice: white pebbles decorate the façade of the Neolithic burial chamber at Newgrange in Ireland. On Man, white pebbles are found in Bronze Age tombs, and they occur in hundreds at keeill sites.

St Patrick's Chair (see overleaf) is in a field in the parish of Marown, near the centre of the southern half of Man. It is thought to be an early Christian preaching station: a site where the gospel was proclaimed before churches were established. Its three slabs are set in a cairn of stones: they may originally have formed a pre-Christian dolmen. At some time between 400 and 700, simple crosses were carved on two of the slabs. The site acquired its name much later: dedications to saints on Man are Norse or medieval. However, missionaries came to the island, perhaps from the time of Ninian (see Chapter Fourteen) onwards, and the names of a few Manx bishops and monks survive on early gravestones.

139. St Patrick's Chair, Marown.

Knock-y-Dooney is a keeill site in the parish of Andreas, on the north-west coast of Man. It is one of three Manx place names which incorporate the word *doonee*, meaning 'Sunday' or 'church'. It is an early word deriving from the Latin *dominica*, which, as we saw in Chapter One, was taken into the Irish language as *domnach*. The word was in use only from about 430 to 550, and is not found in Scotland or Wales. It is likely that its usage spread to Man from Ireland, and that the Manx *doonee* churches were founded by Irish missionaries or emigrants. The first reference to Knock-y-Dooney dates from 1627; the outline of its keeill can still be seen.[2]

Four early gravestones with Latin inscriptions have been discovered on the Isle of Man. One of these comes from Knock-y-Dooney, and is shown in the photograph opposite. It is an early sixth-century pillar stone with an inscription in Irish ogham up one side. The same text is carved in Latin in rusticated Roman capitals, on the broad face of the stone. It reads: 'Ammecatus, son of Rocatus, lies here.' These are names of Irish warriors, so the chapel may have been attached to the fort of a local chieftain. The stone resembles those found in north Wales; the keeill was perhaps founded by missionaries from the well-established Romano-British church in the Conwy Valley.[3]

140. Stone pillar, Knock-y-Dooney.

Later waves of Christians moved into this area of Man. Within a mile of Knock-y-Dooney is Kirk Andreas, built over a keeill dedicated to Columba (see Chapter Seventeen). It may have been founded by monks from his monastery of Iona, off the west coast of Scotland. Later still, the area was populated with Norse Christians, and one of the finest collections of tenth-century Norse cross slabs can be seen at Kirk Andreas. The stonemasons expressed pride in their Scandinavian ancestry by depicting scenes from Norse myths. On one stone, Sigurd the Dragon-slayer roasts the dragon's heart on a spit. Another presents the last great battle between the gods and the forces of hell. An inscription in runes down its edge reads:

> Thorwald erected this cross.
> Then there shall come One yet mightier, though him I dare
>   not name.

A third cross was erected by Sandulf in memory of his wife, who is shown sitting side-saddle on her horse.[4]

Kirk Maughold is on the north-east coast of the island, on a hillside above the sea. The present church dates from the twelfth century, but within the graveyard are the remains of three keeills, and the sites of three more, including two beneath the medieval church. Each had a window of red sandstone and was surrounded by a small cemetery. The foundations of one keeill can be seen in the photograph, with a later well at its south-east corner. Maughold was the principal monastery on the Isle of Man. Its first monks appear to have originated from Northumbria and from Galloway in south-west Scotland. The buildings were probably of timber, like those of Northumbrian monasteries. Many of its monuments were carved by itinerant Anglian stonemasons. Iron ore was mined at Maughold, which enabled metal-working to be carried out. By 795 Vikings had begun to rob exposed places on the coast, and Maughold was an easy target. By about 830 colonists arrived and took possession of the arable land. Without land, the monastery could not continue; for a long period, no further monuments were constructed here. Norsemen buried their dead in the cemetery, for graves contain their weapons, including a sword dating from about 900.

There was a powerful spring on the site, and Norsemen may have named the place *Makt-kelda*, meaning 'forceful spring'.[5] In his *Life of Patrick* (*c.* 1186), a monk named Jocelyn from the Benedictine abbey of Furness described the spring as St Machaldus' well. He linked it with the story of an Irish adventurer told by the seventh-century biographer of Patrick, Muirchú, who described a cruel tyrant named Macc Cuill and his dramatic conversion to a holy life. Macc Cuill normally killed travellers passing through his territory, and when he heard that Patrick was coming, he planned to murder him. Patrick survived, and restored a dead man back to life. The tyrant was converted, declared his belief in God, confessed his sins and asked to do penance. Patrick ordered him to abandon everything and set off in a small boat without oars or a rudder. Macc Cuill was set adrift and arrived at a distant land, where two holy bishops trained him. Eventually he too became a bishop. By telling the story of how a wicked man became a fervent monk, Muirchú presented a model of holy living. It was based on earlier moral tales: Cassian recounts how one of the desert fathers, Abba Moses, began as a murderer but was converted and became a wise and holy monk.[6]

It is considered unlikely that there was a Manx saint named Maughold, but we do gain glimpses of the monks who lived at the monastery from its fine collection of carved stone slabs. The oldest is a memorial to Irneit, a seventh-century monastic bishop. His name is inscribed in a circle surrounding a hexafoil cross. This design, resembling a six-petalled flower, is found in sub-Roman Britain and Gaul, so the stonemason had learnt his skill abroad. A pair of eighth-century stones coming from the head and foot of a grave commemorate someone called Blakman. His name is Saxon, but the style of the cross is Celtic. It shows how Teutonic settlers spread across northern Britain and adopted Celtic culture. Another slab is inscribed in Latin: 'Branhui led off water to this place.' Branhui was a monk with a Welsh name who provided the monastery with its water supply in about 800. Traces of his stone-lined conduit have been found. An early ninth-century cross names a Welsh prince, Guriat,

141. Keeill at Maughold Monastery.

who may have taken refuge on the island before 825. Another cross from the same period depicts two desert fathers who inspired Celtic monks: St Anthony and Paul the Hermit. They sit on solid chairs on either side of a ringed cross, each bearded and dressed in a monk's cowl and hood.[6]

St Patrick's Isle at Peel is situated halfway along the west coast of Man. Until the eighteenth century it was a tidal islet, accessible on foot at low tide. There is now a causeway leading to the island, which is dominated by the medieval cathedral of St German and a later castle. The island was inhabited from early times, and a number of round houses dating from 400 BC have been excavated. These homesteads were very large – up to 10 metres in diameter – and one included a grain store which later burnt down. Their inhabitants grew cereals and raised cattle; they wore textiles, worked metals and traded with the outside world.

Later, there was a Christian community on St Patrick's Isle. Its first buildings have not survived; they would have been small cells of wattle and daub, with a church of heavier timber, and a few more communal buildings. From the seventh century onwards there was an extensive cemetery at the southern end of the island, near the medieval cathedral. The ruins of a church, a chapel and a round tower survive from the Celtic monastery, each dating in part from the tenth century. St Patrick's church was constructed of roughly dressed local red sandstone. It had antae, or side walls projecting beyond the line of the gables; this style of building was common in Ireland. St Patrick's chapel is smaller, but of similar construction.

142. Altar front, Peel.

The photograph shows an altar slab that was found when the two buildings were restored in 1873. It is decorated with five small crosses set within a larger one, and formed the front panel of a stone altar. Near St Patrick's church is a squat round tower, 15 metres high. Four windows facing the compass points near the top indicate that this was its original height. It, too, is built of red sandstone; its battlemented parapet was added in about 1600. Lintel graves and crosses dating from the seventh and eighth centuries were found beneath the south transept of St German's cathedral.

The monastery was ravaged by Viking raiders, and the little island became a base for Norse settlers. They built a fort of timber or pile, which gave Peel its name. Excavations beneath Peel castle have produced evidence of at least seven pagan burials within the Christian cemetery. The richest grave was that of a Viking woman who was interred with her cooking spit: this was a symbol of domestic power in Scandinavia. At her side were her knives and sewing equipment, including a workbox, needle and shears. She wore a magnificent necklace of seventy-three glass, amber and jet beads, some already centuries old. The burial of a wealthy pagan Norsewoman in a Christian cemetery reflects the mixture of material cultures and beliefs that have shaped the Manx people.

Lag ny Keeilley, or 'hollow of the chapel' is in Patrick parish on the south-west coast of Man. It is in a beautiful location, where hills fall steeply to the sea and seals play around the rocks. It can be reached by walking over a kilometre along a track from Eary Cushlin car park. In earlier times, this was the packhorse road to the south of the island. People continued to bring their dead along the track for burial at Lag ny Keeilley until about 1800. An elderly parishioner from Eary Cushlin recalled how the corpse would be wrapped in a winding sheet and strapped to the back of an old mare, supported by a bundle of straw which served as a saddle. The horse was led down the long track to the little burial ground surrounding the keeill.[7]

The solitary monk who founded the keeill had levelled the enclosure with considerable effort by digging into the hillside and building up a level platform. Within a retaining embankment he constructed his chapel and his house. The keeill is 4 metres long and 2.65 metres wide. Its altar survives; a pear-shaped stone that had been brought up the steep track from the beach formed one of its supporting pillars. Above the altar was a window with a carved sandstone head. A slab of local slate with a hollow cup in one corner was probably a cresset, containing oil and a wick for a lamp. Some flat stones survive from the original pavement, as does the stone socket for a door in the west wall.[8] This is a unique feature: there is no sign of a door at other keeills. Many are thought to have been closed by a *scraa*, or bundle of willow shoots with a heather band around the middle. A stick twisted into the band would catch the wall on either side and block the entrance.

Near the keeill are remains of a rectangular stone dwelling for the priest, with a small garden plot. A piece of a granite quern found near the keeill may indicate that the priest baked bread. In Ireland, however, those caught grinding corn on a Sunday brought their quern to the church, and smashed it as part of their penance. The same

143. The Well of Baptism, Lag ny Keeilley.

144. Linen drying on a fuchsia hedge, Cregneash.

may have been true on Man, since quern fragments are common at keeill sites. The burial ground contains stone-lined lintel graves and some simple slate crosses. About six hundred white quartz pebbles were found in and near the keeill, suggesting that it continued as a place of pilgrimage.[9] Near the end of the packhorse road, almost within sight of the keeill, is a well known as *Chibbyr ny Vashtey* in Manx, or 'The Well of Baptism' (see p. 200). It was visited for healing until recent times.

There are records of 174 keeills on the Isle of Man. Thirty-five of these can still be identified, although most of their remains date from Norse times or later. When roofed, they would have resembled the cottage in the photograph on the previous page, apart from its chimney: the roof was thatched with reeds and bound by ropes to pegs fixed in the walls. Altar linen would be washed and hung on bushes to dry. No liturgical manuscripts survive, but the Manx name for the feast of the Epiphany on 6 January is 'Festival of the Water Well'. The Epiphany is a feast of water and a day for baptism in the Eastern Churches but not in the Roman rite, so the Manx name may survive from Celtic times.[10]

Many of the keeills are built using a primitive drystone technique: their walls are often a metre thick, with stone facing on the two surfaces and a filling of earth and small stones. Many of these chapels date from the eighth and ninth centuries. Some, like that of Druidale in the upper valley of the River Sulby, on the shoulder of Snaefell, are built near summer shielings, and would not have been used in winter. While some keeills were in settlements, others were more isolated. Patrick's Chapel at Spooyt Vane, just south of Kirk Michael on the west coast, is in a wooded glade close to a waterfall, beside a river. Outside the small enclosure was a hut where the priest lived, and a well. Converts could be baptised beneath the white waterfall (or *spooyt vane* in Manx) that gave the settlement its name.

Most Manx place names derive from Old Norse. This suggests that Vikings took possession of all the useful land. However, most of these adventurers seem to have been unmarried when they arrived. The Gaelic-speaking inhabitants were dispossessed but not annihilated, and they intermarried with the newcomers. By the end of the tenth century, Gaelic and Norse names are recorded together on gravestones. It is likely that Church organisation was destroyed by the Norse invaders, and priests were driven off their church sites. By the mid-tenth century, pre-Norse churches had been in ruins for over a hundred years. The Christian culture of the later Norse settlers formed the foundation of the medieval Church on Man.

CONCLUSION

What was it like to be an early British man or woman of God? The Celtic saints were remarkable travellers and fearless missionaries, but neither travelling nor preaching was their primary aim. They saw themselves as pilgrims for the love of God, and set out from their homeland to a place that God would show them, a place where they could be free from family ties and tribal responsibilities. In the Old Testament, God had called Abraham in a similar way. The Book of Genesis recounts that Abraham was living in Mesopotamia when he heard God say: 'Leave your country, your family and your father's house, for the land I will show you. I will make you a great nation.'[1] Early British Christians were familiar with this story, and many of them felt drawn by a similar call.

The Breton monk who wrote the *Life of Samson* (see Chapter Nineteen) describes the bishop receiving a call like that of Abraham, in similar words. One Easter night, Samson celebrated the great Vigil liturgy for the monks of his monastery: he lit the Easter fire, blessed the new baptismal water and celebrated Eucharist. Afterwards, he stayed behind in the church to pray, while the other monks went back to their cells to sleep. As Samson prayed, an angel appeared to him saying, 'Rejoice, saint of God. . . . For I am sent to you from my Lord. You must remain here in your country no longer. You are destined to be a pilgrim. Beyond the sea, you will be very great in the Church.'[2]. The author portrays Samson completing the Easter services, packing at once, and setting sail. En route 'he visited his mother and aunt (in south-east Wales) and consecrated their churches, which were now built. . . . He rejoiced to find his brothers and cousins leading a noble Christian life with their mothers.'[3]

Writing in the late seventh century, Abbot Adomnán of Iona describes Columba's call in similar language: 'From his boyhood he had been devoted to the service of Christ and the pursuit of wisdom. By God's gift he preserved both integrity of body and purity of soul. . . . In the second year after the battle of Cul-drebene, aged forty-two, Columba sailed from Ireland to Britain, wishing to become a pilgrim for Christ.'[4] As we saw in Chapter Seventeen, there were other strands to Columba's life, and other motives for his journeying, but his biographer highlights the values that both he and Columba held dear.

Adomnán's description of Columba's final days focuses on further qualities that were prized by early British Christians: a simple life of love, peace and prayer. Although ill, Columba sang Vespers for Saturday evening in church with his brother monks. He returned to his hut, where he normally slept on a rock slab with a stone for a pillow, but that night he felt too ill to sleep, and sat on his bed. Adomnán comments that Columba's pillow stone still stood by his grave as a memorial to the great man. The author records Columba's simple speech to his monks: 'These are my last words to you, my children: keep mutual and genuine love and peace among yourselves. . . . And not only will God provide all you need for this present life, but he will also give you the reward of eternal riches.'[5]

Having set out as exiles for God, like so many of their fellow Christians, Samson and Columba each found the place that God revealed to them. They lacked nothing, and looked forward to their birth into heavenly life. Adomnán is not modest about such an achievement. So greatly was Columba blessed, wrote Adomnán, that 'although he lived in this small and remote island of the British sea (Iona), the merit of his name has spread not only throughout the whole of our land of Ireland and throughout Britain, that is the largest island in the whole world. His fame has gone forth even as far as triangular Spain, to Gaul and to Italy, which lies beyond the Apennine Alps. Yes, it has even reached the greatest of cities, Rome.'[6] Early British Christians were proud of the values they held dear, values that they took with them as they travelled throughout the entire known world.

NOTES

Place of publication is London unless stated otherwise

INTRODUCTION

1. Athanasius, 'The Life of Antony' in *Patrologia Graeca*, ed. J.P. Migne (Paris, 1857–66), vol. 36, columns 835–978

2. Sulpicius Severus, 'The Life of Martin of Tours' in *Patrologia Latina*, ed. J.P. Migne (Paris, 1844–64), vol. 20, columns 159–222

CHAPTER ONE

1. Recent translations of Patrick's *Confession* are found in T. O'Loughlin, *St Patrick: The Man and His Works* (SPCK, 1999) and J. Skinner, *The Confession of St Patrick* (New York, Doubleday, 1998)

2. Patrick's *Letter to Coroticus* is found in O'Loughlin, *St Patrick*, pp. 93–105 and in Skinner, *The Confession*, pp. 1–16

3. Patrick, *Confession*, 16

4. Ibid., 46

5. T. O'Loughlin, *Journeys to the Edges: The Celtic Tradition* (Darton, Longman & Todd, 2000), pp. 88–90

6. Patrick, *Confession*, pp. 51, 14

7. Ibid., p. 38

8. Ibid., pp. 41, 42

9. Ibid., p. 40

10. Ibid., p. 43

11. Ibid., p. 55

12. Ibid., pp. 61, 62

13. D. McRoberts, *The Chapel of Saint Mahew*, Cardross (Edinburgh, Constable, 1955), pp. 5–7

CHAPTER TWO

1. R. Sharpe, *Medieval Irish Saints' Lives: an Introduction to* Vitae Sanctorum Hiberniae (Oxford University Press, 1991), p. 243

2. C. Thomas, *And Shall These Mute Stones Speak?* (Cardiff, University of Wales Press, 1994), pp. 33–4

3. S. Lincoln, *Declan of Ardmore* (Cork, Aisling, 1995), p. 32

4. Ibid., p. 43

5. Ibid., p. 32

CHAPTER THREE

1. C. Manning, *Early Irish Monasteries* (Dublin, Town House & Country House, 1995), pp. 16, 29

2. A. Carmichael, *Carmina Gadelica* (Edinburgh, Floris, 1992), nos 101, 130, 263, 264, 323, 368

3. Ibid., pp. 580–2

4. E. Rees, *Christian Symbols, Ancient Roots* (Jessica Kingsley, 1992), pp. 28–31

5. Carmichael, *Carmina Gadelica*, pp. 582–6

6. Ibid., p. 582

7. W.J. Watson, *The History of the Celtic Place-names of Scotland* (Edinburgh, Birlinn, 1993), p. 275

8. G. Webster, *The British Celts and their Gods under Rome* (Batsford, 1986), p. 32

9. M. Costen, *The Origins of Somerset* (Manchester University Press, 1992), p. 46

CHAPTER FOUR

1. C. Manning, *Clonmacnoise* (Dublin, Dúchas, 1998), p. 52

2. C. Manning, *Early Irish Monasteries* (Dublin, Town House & Country House, 1995), p. 24

3. J. Marsden, *The Illustrated Columcille* (Macmillan, 1991), p. 60

4. Manning, *Clonmacnoise*, p. 7

5. Ibid., p. 36

CHAPTER FIVE

1. L. Barrow, *Glendalough and St Kevin* (Dundalk, Dundalgan Press, 1992), pp. 16–17

2. C. Manning, *Early Irish Monasteries* (Dublin, Town House & Country House, 1995), pp. 30, 36

3. Barrow, *Glendalough*, pp. 11–12

4. Ibid., pp. 38–40

5. Ibid., p. 24

CHAPTER SIX

1. W. J. Watson, *The History of the Celtic Place-names of Scotland* (Edinburgh, Birlinn, 1993), p. 274

2. There is a summary of the *Navigatio* in Appendix I of Tim Severin's account of his re-creation of Brendan's epic journey: *The Brendan Voyage* (New York, McGraw-Hill, 1978), pp. 265–73

3. Luke 14:26

4. Genesis 6–8

5. E. Rees, *Christian Symbols, Ancient Roots* (Jessica Kingsley, 1992), pp. 40–1

6. Matthew 8:25

7. T. O'Loughlin, *Journeys on the Edges: the Celtic Tradition* (Darton, Longman & Todd, 2000), pp. 91–8

8. Revelation 21:23

9. Matthew 25:13

10. P. Harbison, *Ancient Irish Monuments* (Dublin, Gill & Macmillan, 1997), pp. 33–5

CHAPTER SEVEN

1. M. Low, *Celtic Christianity and Nature* (Belfast, Black Star Press, 1996), p. 158

2. I Kings 18:20–40

3. T. O'Loughlin, *Journeys on the Edges: the Celtic Tradition* (Darton, Longman & Todd, 2000), pp. 101–10

4. C. Manning, *Early Irish Monasteries* (Dublin, Town House & Country House, 1995), pp. 22–3

5. J.P. Hynes, *Kilmacduagh: a Short Guide* (Mold, J.P. Hynes, 1986), p. 8

6. Ibid., p. 9

CHAPTER EIGHT

1. E. G. Bowen, *The St David of History. Dewi Sant: Our Founder Saint* (Aberystwyth, Friends of St David's Cathedral, 1982), pp. 9–10

2. F. Jones, *The Holy Wells of Wales* (Cardiff, University of Wales Press, 1992), p. 27

3. Bowen, *The St David of History*, pp. 15–16

4. Jones, *The Holy Wells of Wales*, p. 69

5. R. Fenton, *Historical Tour through Pembrokeshire* (Brecknock, Fenton, 1903), pp. 63–4

6. Bowen, *The St David of History*, pp. 11–13

7. O. Davies, *Celtic Christianity in Early Medieval Wales: The Origins of the Welsh Spiritual Tradition* (Cardiff, University of Wales Press, 1996), p. 23

8. Bowen, *The St David of History*, pp. 7–8

9. R. van der Weyer, *Celtic Fire: an Anthology of Christian Literature* (Darton, Longman & Todd, 1990), pp. 70–1

10. Davies, *Celtic Christianity in Medieval Wales*, pp. 45–8

11. van der Weyer, *Celtic Fire*, pp. 71–2

12. J. Meyrick, *A Pilgrim's Guide to the Holy Wells of Cornwall* (Falmouth, Meyrick, 1982), p. 15

13. N. Orme, *The Saints of Cornwall* (Oxford University Press, 2000), pp. 207–8

14. Meyrick, *A Pilgrim's Guide*, pp. 119–20

CHAPTER NINE

1. E. Rees, *Celtic Saints, Passionate Wanderers* (Thames & Hudson, 2000), pp. 18–0

2. A. Muir, R. Paterson and R. Jones, *The Story of St Catwg's Church, Langattock* (Langattock Parish Council, 1991), p. 7

3. H. Dudley, *The Parish Church of St Stephen and St Tathan, Caerwent* (Caerwent Parish Council, 1990), pp. 2–3

4. B. Colgrave and R.A. Mynors (eds), *Bede's Ecclesiastical History of the English People* (Oxford University Press, 1969), Bk 1, ch. 7

5. Rees, *Celtic Saints*, pp. 12–13

6. Ibid.

CHAPTER TEN

1. E.G. Bowen, *The Settlements of the Celtic Saints in Wales* (Cardiff, University of Wales Press, 1954), p. 83

2. F. Jones, *The Holy Wells of Wales* (Cardiff, University of Wales Press, 1992), p. 178

3. D. Gregory, *Country Churchyards in Wales* (Llanwrst, Gwasg Carreg Gwalch, 1991), p. 74

4. Ibid., p. 76

5. Jones, *The Holy Wells of Wales*, pp. 108, 179

6. Gregory, *Country Churchyards*, p. 76

CHAPTER ELEVEN

1. C. David, *St Winefride's Well: a History and Guide* (Kildare, Leinster Leader, 1993), p. 5

2. F. Jones, *The Holy Wells of Wales* (Cardiff, University of Wales Press, 1992), p. 174

3. P. Caraman (trans), *The Hunted Priest: Autobiography of John Gerard* (Collins Fontana, 1959), p. 62

4. David, *St Winefride's Well*, pp. 20, 22

5. D. Gregory, *Country Churchyards in Wales* (Llanwrst, Gwasg Carreg Gwalch, 1991), pp. 39, 63

6. T. Roberts, 'Welsh Ecclesiastical Place-names and Archaeology' in N. Edwards and A. Lane (eds), *The Early Church in Wales and the West*, Oxbow Monographs no. 16 (Oxford, Oxbow Books, 1992), p. 43

7. A. Chetan and D. Brueton, *The Sacred Yew* (Penguin Arkana, 1994), pp. 55, 153

8. E. Peters, *Cadfael: A Morbid Taste for Bones* (Warner Futura, 1977)

9. N. Edwards and A. Lane, 'Archaeology of the Early Church in Wales: An Introduction' in Edwards and Lane, *The Early Church in Wales and the West*, pp. 9–10

10. J. Bord and C. Bord, *Sacred Waters: Holy Wells and Water Lore in Britain and Ireland* (Paladin, 1986), p. 206

11. Ibid., p. 96

CHAPTER TWELVE

1. F. Jones, *The Holy Wells of Wales* (Cardiff, University of Wales Press, 1992), p. 191

2. M. Chitty, *The Monks on Ynys Enlli*, Part 1, c. 500 AD – 1252 AD (Aberdaron, Mary Chitty, 1992), pp. 13–14

3. Ibid., pp. 14–15

4. P.H. Jones, *Bardsey, Its History and Wildlife* (Criccieth, Bardsey Island Trust, 1995), p. 10

5. Chitty, *The Monks of Ynys Enlli*, pp. 21–22

6. Jones, *The Holy Wells of Wales*, p. 152

7. Chitty, *The Monks of Ynys Enlli*, p. 15

8. E.G. Bowen, *The Settlements of the Celtic Saints in Wales* (Cardiff, University of Wales Press, 1954), p. 95

9. Jones, *The Holy Wells of Wales*, pp. 116, 190

10. C. Knightly, *Mwynhewch Sir Ddinbych Ganoloesol* (Denbigh, Cyngor Sir Ddinbych, 1998), p. 18

11. Jones, *The Holy Wells of Wales*, p. 178

CHAPTER THIRTEEN

1. B. Colgrave and R.A. Mynors (eds), *Bede's Ecclesiastical History of the English People* (Oxford University Press, 1969), Bk 2, ch. 2

2.   Ibid.

3.   W.P. Seymour Davies, *The History of the Church of St Tysilio and St Mary, Meifod* (Welshpool, Meifod Parish Council, 1984), p. 7

4.   Ibid., p. 4

5.   D. Senogles, *A History of Part of the Parish of Llandysilio* (Llanfairpwllgwyngyll, Landysilio Parish Council, 1997), pp. 3-4

6.   D. Allchin, 'Where the Saints Have Trod', *Church Times*, 7 August 1998

CHAPTER FOURTEEN

1.   B. Colgrave and R. A. Mynors (eds), *Bede's Ecclesiastical History of the English People* (Oxford University Press, 1969), Bk 3, ch. 4

2.   A full account of the excavations at Whithorn is found in P. Hill, *Whithorn and St Ninian: the Excavation of a Monastic Town 1984–91* (Stroud, Sutton Publishing, 1997)

3.   W.J. Watson, *The History of the Celtic Place-names of Scotland* (Edinburgh, Birlinn, 1986), p. 160

4.   I. MacDonald (ed.), *Saint Ninian, by Aelred, Abbot of Rievaulx* (Edinburgh, Floris, 1993)

5.   Cumberland and Westmoreland Antiquarian Society, 'Saint Martin's Church, Brampton', in *Transactions of the Cumberland and Westmoreland Antiquarian Society*, vol. 82, 1982

6.   Ibid.

7.   E. Rees, *Celtic Saints, Passionate Wanderers* (Thames & Hudson, 2000), p. 92

8.   Watson, *Celtic Place-names of Scotland*, p. 294

9.   MacDonald, *Saint Ninian*, pp. 31–3

10. Watson, *Celtic Place-names of Scotland*, p. 159

CHAPTER FIFTEEN

1.   J. Sinclair, *St Mackessog's Church, Luss, Loch Lomond* (Loch Lomond, Luss Church Promotions, n.d.), p. 1

2.   *Gerard's Herbal*, 1636, ed. M. Woodward (London, Bracken Books, 1985), pp. 19–20

3.   I. Zaczek, *Ancient Scotland* (London, Collins and Brown, 1998), p. 84

4.   D. Smith, *Celtic Travellers: Scotland in the Age of the Saints* (Edinburgh, Stationery Office, 1997), p. 12

5.   W.J. Watson, *The History of the Celtic Place-names of Scotland* (Edinburgh, Birlinn, 1986), p. 278

6.   Adomnán, 'Prophecy Concerning Artbranan' in J. Marsden, *The Illustrated Columcille* (Macmillan, 1991), p. 78

7.   Sinclair, *St Mackessog's Church*, p. 1

8.   Watson, *Celtic Place-names of Scotland*, p. 278

CHAPTER SIXTEEN

1.   I. MacDonald (ed), *Saint Mungo, Also Known as Kentigern, by Jocelinus, a Monk of Furness* (Edinburgh, Floris, 1993), pp. 11–12

2.   P. Sked, *Culross* (Edinburgh, National Trust for Scotland, 1994), pp. 20, 23

3.   MacDonald, *Saint Mungo*, pp. 29–30

4.   E. Rees, *Celtic Saints, Passionate Wanderers* (Thames and Hudson, 2000), p. 96

5.   MacDonald, *Saint Mungo*, pp. 31, 34

6.   Ibid., pp. 32–4

7.   Ibid., pp. 36–7, 42–3

8.   J. Griffiths, *A Short Guide to the Parish Church of St Asaph and St Cyndeyrn, Llanasa* (Llanasa, A5 Publications, 1986), pp. 1–2, 5

9.   MacDonald, *Saint Mungo*, pp. 41–6

CHAPTER SEVENTEEN

1.   D. Smith, *Celtic Travellers: Scotland in the Age of the Saints* (Edinburgh, Stationery Office, 1997), p. 15

2.   J. Dunbar and I. Fisher, *Iona: a Guide to the Monuments* (Edinburgh, Her Majesty's Stationery Office, 1995), p. 15

3.   E. Rees, *Celtic Saints, Passionate Wanderers* (Thames & Hudson, 2000), pp. 108–9

4.   Dunbar and Fisher, *Iona*, p. 13.

5.   Ibid., p. 15

6.   Ibid., p. 27

7.   J. Marsden, *The Illustrated Columcille* (Macmillan, 1991), p. 38

8.   Ibid., p. 120

9.   Smith, *Celtic Travellers*, p. 10

10. Marsden, *Illustrated Columcille*, pp. 172–4

11. B. Colgrave, and R.A. Mynors (eds), *Bede's Ecclesiastical History of the English People* (Oxford University Press, 1969), Bk 5, ch. 25

12. E. G. Bowen, *Saints, Seaways and Settlements in the Celtic Lands* (Cardiff, University of Wales Press, 1969), p. 25

CHAPTER EIGHTEEN

1. D.H. Farmer, *The Oxford Dictionary of Saints* (Oxford University Press, 1984), p. 90
2. D. Smith, *Celtic Travellers: Scotland in the Age of the Saints* (Edinburgh, Stationery Office, 1997), p. 12
3. E. Rees, *Celtic Saints, Passionate Wanderers* (Thames & Hudson, 2000), pp. 117–18
4. Smith, *Celtic Travellers*, p. 30
5. Ibid.

CHAPTER NINETEEN

1. J. Meyrick, *A Pilgrim's Guide to the Holy Wells of Cornwall* (Falmouth, Meyrick, 1982), p. 67
2. 'The Life of Samson', ch. 46 in D. Attwater (ed.), *The Saints of Cornwall by G. Doble* (Truro, 1960–70) vol. 5, p. 87
3. Ibid., chs 48–9, pp. 87–8
4. Ibid., ch. 50, pp. 88–9
5. Ibid., ch. 51, p. 89
6. C. Thomas, *And Shall These Mute Stones Speak?* (Cardiff, University of Wales Press, 1994), pp. 61–4

CHAPTER TWENTY

1. C. Thomas, *And Shall These Mute Stones Speak?* (Cardiff, University of Wales Press, 1994), pp. 145–51
2. N. Orme, *The Saints of Cornwall* (Oxford University Press, 2000), p. 198
3. N. Johnson and P. Rose, *Cornwall's Archaeological Heritage* (Truro, Cornwall Archaeological Unit, 1990), p. 40
4. J. Meyrick, *A Pilgrim's Guide to the Holy Wells of Cornwall* (Falmouth, Meyrick, 1982), p. 60
5. Orme, *The Saints of Cornwall*, p. 113
6. Ibid., p. 89
7. R. Gradwell, *St Clether Holy Well* (Camelford, n.d.), p. 3

8. Orme, *The Saints of Cornwall*, p. 162
9. Ibid., p. 163

CHAPTER TWENTY-ONE

1. N. Orme, *The Saints of Cornwall* (Oxford University Press, 2000), p. 215
2. Ibid., pp. 214-17
3. J. Meyrick, *A Pilgrim's Guide to the Holy Wells of Cornwall* (Falmouth, Meyrick, 1982), pp. 99–100
4. Orme, *The Saints of Cornwall*, p. 131
5. Meyrick, *A Pilgrim's Guide*, p. 21
6. J. Chapman, *St Petroc* (Bodmin, Chapman, 1995), pp. 4–5
7. Orme, *The Saints of Cornwall*, pp. 218–19
8. Ibid., p. 219

CHAPTER TWENTY-TWO

1. C. Thomas, *And Shall These Mute Stones Speak?* (Cardiff, University of Wales Press, 1994), p. 291
2. F. Jones, *The Holy Wells of Wales* (Cardiff, University of Wales Press, 1992), p. 94
3. N. Orme, *The Saints of Cornwall* (Oxford University Press, 2000), pp. 169–71
4. J. Meyrick, *A Pilgrim's Guide to the Holy Wells of Cornwall* (Falmouth, Meyrick, 1982), p. 79
5. Orme, *The Saints of Cornwall*, p. 212
6. Ibid, p. 234
7. E. Rees, *Christian Symbols, Ancient Roots* (Jessica Kingsley, 1992), p. 28
8. Meyrick, *A Pilgrim's Guide*, p. 71
9. Orme, *The Saints of Cornwall*, pp.100–1
10. Meyrick, *A Pilgrim's Guide*, p. 36
11. Ibid., p. 130
12. Orme, *The Saints of Cornwall*, pp. 226–7

CHAPTER TWENTY-THREE

1. B. Colgrave and R.A. Mynors (eds), *Bede's Ecclesiastical History of the English People* (Oxford University Press, 1969), Bk 3, ch. 5

2. Ibid., ch. 3
3. Ibid., ch.5
4. Ibid., ch. 6
5. J. Bord and C. Bord, *Sacred Waters: Holy Wells and Water Lore in Britain and Ireland* (Paladin, 1986), pp. 20, 122, 205–6
6. Colgrave and Mynors, *Bede*, Bk 3, ch. 9
7. Ibid., ch. 14
8. Ibid.
9. Ibid., ch. 5
10. Ibid., ch. 17
11. Ibid., ch. 16
12. J. Bird, *St Aidan's Church, Bamburgh, and its Story through 1400 Years* (Bamburgh, John Bird, 1985), pp. 5–8

CHAPTER TWENTY-FOUR

1. Bede, 'The Life and Miracles of St Cuthbert' ch.6, in B. Colgrave and R.A. Mynors (eds), *The Ecclesiastical History of the English People* (Oxford University Press, 1969)
2. Ibid., chs. 9, 11
3. D. Smith, *Celtic Travellers: Scotland in the Age of the Saints* (Edinburgh, Stationery Office, 1997), p. 30
4. Bede, *Life and Miracles of St Cuthbert*, ch. 8
5. Ibid., ch. 16
6. Ibid.
7. E. Cambridge, *Lindisfarne Priory and Holy Island* (English Heritage, 1995), p. 15
8. Ibid., p. 14
9. Bede, *Life and Miracles of St Cuthbert*, chs. 17, 18, 20
10. Ibid., ch. 19
11. Ibid., ch. 18
12. Ibid., ch. 36
13. Ibid., ch. 27
14. Ibid., chs 39, 40

CHAPTER TWENTY-FIVE

1. R. Geddes, 'The Isle of Man' in *Celtic Saints: Passionate Wanderers*, E. Rees (Thames & Hudson, 2000), p. 155
2. D.S. Dugdale, *Manx Church Origins* (Lampeter, Llanerch, 1998), pp. 20–3
3. Ibid., pp. 24–5
4. A.M. Cubbon, *The Art of Manx Crosses* (Douglas, Manx Museum and National Trust, 1977), pp. 22–3, 29, 32–3
5. Dugdale, *Manx Church Origins*, p. 62, 113–15
6. T. O'Loughlin, *Journeys on the Edges: the Celtic Tradition* (Darton, Longman & Todd, 2000), pp. 90–1
7. W.C. Corlett, W.K. Kermode, P. Cadman *et al.*, *Annual Report of the Manx Archaeological Society* (1909), p. 19
8. Ibid., pp. 20–5
9. Ibid., pp. 23–6
10. Dugdale, *Manx Church Origins*, p. 190

CONCLUSION

1. Genesis 12:1–2
2. 'The Life of Samson' in D. Attwater (ed.), *The Saints of Cornwall by G. Doble* (Truro, 1960–70) vol. 5, p. 86
3. Ibid.
4. Preface to Adomnán's *Life of Columba*, translation based on J. Marsden, *The Illustrated Columcille* (Macmillan, 1991), p. 56; I. MacDonald, *St Columba* (Edinburgh, Floris, 1992), p. 12
5. Adomnán's *Life of Columba* in Marsden, p. 172, and MacDonald, p. 56
6. Ibid., Marsden, p. 175, and MacDonald, p. 62

INDEX